Youth
BASEBALL
Drills

Marty Schupak

HUMAN KINETICS

Library of Congress Cataloging-in-Publication Data

Schupak, Marty.
  Youth baseball drills / Marty Schupak.
    p. cm.
  ISBN 0-7360-5632-7 (soft cover)
  1. Baseball for children--Training. 2. Baseball for children--Coaching. I. Title.
  GV880.4.S38 2005
  796.357'62--dc22

                                                      2004028229

ISBN-10: 0-7360-5632-7
ISBN-13: 978-0-7360-5632-8

The Web addresses cited in this text were current as of November 2, 2004 unless otherwise noted.

Developmental Editor: Kase Johnstun; **Assistant Editors:** Cory Weber and Carla Zych; **Copyeditor:** Annette Pierce; **Proofreader:** Erin Cler; **Graphic Designer:** Robert Reuther; **Graphic Artist:** Tara Welsch; **Photo Manager:** Dan Wendt; **Cover Designer:** Keith Blomberg; **Photographer (cover):** ©Bryan Curtis/Gameface Sports Photography; **Photographer (interior):** page 1 ©SportsChrome/Ellen R. Shupp; pages 21, 101, 119, 137, 163, and 189 ©Human Kinetics; page 67 ©Bruce Coleman, Inc.; **Art Manager:** Kareema McLendon; **Illustrator:** Argosy; **Printer:** United Graphics

Human Kinetics books are available at special discounts for bulk purchase. Special editions or book excerpts can also be created to specification. For details, contact the Special Sales Manager at Human Kinetics.

Printed in the United States of America   10 9 8 7

The paper in this book is certified under a sustainable forestry program.

Human Kinetics
Web site: www.HumanKinetics.com

United States: Human Kinetics
P.O. Box 5076
Champaign, IL 61825-5076
800-747-4457
e-mail: humank@hkusa.com

Canada: Human Kinetics
475 Devonshire Road, Unit 100
Windsor, ON N8Y 2L5
800-465-7301 (in Canada only)
e-mail: info@hkcanada.com

Europe: Human Kinetics
107 Bradford Road
Stanningley
Leeds LS28 6AT, United Kingdom
+44 (0)113 255 5665
e-mail: hk@hkeurope.com

Australia: Human Kinetics
57A Price Avenue
Lower Mitcham, South Australia 5062
08 8372 0999
e-mail: info@hkaustralia.com

New Zealand: Human Kinetics
P.O. Box 80
Torrens Park, South Australia 5062
0800 222 062
e-mail: info@hknewzealand.com

Acknowledgments

I'd like to acknowledge the following people who have given me great support over the years, have been patient with my love for youth sports, and have had a part directly or indirectly in the completion of this book: Mike Craven and Thomas Craven Films, Stanly Goldstein, Greg Mitchell, Leonard Kaye, Dr. Robert Pangrazi, Ed Wallace, and Mary Wallace.

I'd like to thank Lennon Nersesian, who was invaluable in the editing process. A special thanks goes to my two brothers, Howard and Paul Schupak, who covered for me at work while I snuck out for baseball practice.

Thanks to my parents, who probably let me stay out too long playing ball during my youth when I should have been inside studying.

I also have to acknowledge all the dedicated parents who coach for the right reasons, volunteer their time, carry equipment bags, drive kids home, eat late fast-food or pizza dinners, and answer phone calls at 10 o'clock at night, only to hear how they coached the game wrong.

Finally, I would like to dedicate this book to my wife, Elaine, and my three children, Jeffrey, Michael, and Lisa. They have been the best infield to ever back me up.

Contents

Introduction   **vii**

1

Throwing Drills **1**

2

Fielding Drills **21**

3

Hitting Drills 67

4

Pitching Drills 101

5

Baserunning Drills 119

6 Game Situation Drills 137

7 Warm-Up and Cool-Down Drills 163

8 Sample Practices 189

Introduction

When I was a graduate student at Arizona State University, one of my professors gave the class some words of wisdom I have never forgotten. He said, "Never confuse activity with accomplishment." His point was that many people keep themselves busy; however, they don't accomplish a heck of a lot.

Jump ahead several years to me watching my son's youth baseball practice. The practice consists of about two and a half hours of batting, during which most of the players appear bored and either swat flies or throw dirt at each other to keep busy. After that practice, I decided to become involved in Little League and to make a concerted effort to keep my practices from being boring or unproductive. I began to research and observe youth baseball practices. I studied different practices from different leagues and learned which skills and drills were effective for each age group. I found that the common element in effective practices is actively involving every player in the drills at the same time.

When designing a youth baseball practice, I strive for two things. First, my practices are rarely much longer than an hour and 15 minutes; therefore, the practices are spirited, and I have the attention of most of the players throughout. Second, I always use a warm-up or cool-down drill to break up a series of skill drills or to end practice on a high note. And I try to relate these drills to the particular baseball fundamental stressed at practice. Warm-up and cool-down drills (see chapter 7) are surprisingly effective for any age group during playoff and all-star time because they can relieve the monotony or staleness of a tedious practice and help the players relax.

The purpose of this book is to teach coaches how to make baseball practices fun while improving the skill level of the players. Most coaching parents also work a full day and therefore find it difficult to make the preparations necessary for a successful season.

However, this book has done much of the legwork for coaches and provides the preparation they need for productive practices. The parent–coaches who use the drills need not be experts in every aspect of the game. However, coaches should know the fundamentals and be able to convey them in a way that allows the players to have fun while learning. These drills, if performed with discipline in an organized and efficient manner, serve the dual purpose of being instructional and fun. This isn't to say that every drill must be fun, but practices should include a variety of drills.

The drills in this book are appropriate for players between the ages of 7 and 12. The book is divided into eight chapters that encompass most of the aspects of youth baseball. Chapters 1 through 5 teach drills that address the basic skills of the game: throwing, fielding, hitting, pitching, and baserunning. Chapter 6 includes numerous game situations that teams should practice. Chapter 7 takes you through team games and warm-up and cool-down drills that provide a fun break during practice. I recommend that coaches include one or two warm-up or cool-down drills per practice. Chapter 8 groups the drills into specific sample practices that coaches can use during the season and includes indoor and parking-lot practices. Chapter 8 also offers coaching tips for a smooth season.

Some drills focus on specific positions or don't involve the whole team at once. When you use these drills, adopt the "station" method of coaching. Setting up different stations and using assistant coaches or parents to lead a different drill or activity at each guarantees that players won't stand around doing nothing for long periods of time.

I encourage coaches to change drills or games to fit their team's needs. Also, try to add 5 to 10 new drills each year that you create yourself.

With the immense growth of youth sports and the advent of longer seasons, many youth players are overcoached and undertaught. I have learned that it is better to undercoach kids than to overcoach them. A player is better off mastering four or five basic skills than being confused and burdened by trying to learn too many. I have always held to the same three goals. I want players to (1) improve as individuals, (2) improve as a team, and (3) have fun!

1

Throwing Drills

Throwing drills are among coaches' most popular drills because they don't require a regular playing field and most of them include all the players at once. These drills maximize both space and time.

Throwing is a complicated motion. Some kids seem to learn it naturally, and others need lots of practice to master it. Common mistakes by young players are throwing from the ear (short arm), not following through, or throwing with just the arm rather than using the whole body. It is important to teach young players proper throwing form because it gets more difficult to correct their technique as they get older. The drills in this chapter teach players the proper steps for throwing a baseball, from the grip to the follow-through.

Coaches should stress correct mechanics over throwing accuracy. Important elements to look for in proper throwing mechanics are (1) bringing the arm behind the head rather than starting the throw at the ear, (2) using the whole body including the legs and hips rather than confining the throwing motion to the upper body, and (3) holding the ball with the fingers on top rather than gripping it using various hand positions. There are many other things to look for when assessing throwing motion; however, coaches and parents of young players should concentrate on these three.

Some of the following throwing drills and the pitching drills in chapter 4 help players become familiar with the parts of the body that are involved in the throwing motion. Practicing the throwing motion without a ball or with their eyes closed also helps players become more aware of and comfortable with using the whole body when throwing. Practicing with soft-covered balls, which are used in leagues throughout the country, not only provides safety but also allows teams the flexibility to practice on unconventional baseball surfaces, such as parking lots or inside gyms.

The arm strength of players 7 to 12 years old varies greatly from year to year. Even a player's arm strength during the course of a four- or five-month season can improve significantly depending on a growth spurt.

Many coaches will have only the pitcher do certain throwing drills. Having the whole team practice pitching drills, including throwing from the pitcher's mound, will help with players' overall throwing mechanics. Coaches are also encouraged to give a general education on throwing to parents; many will play catch with their kids, and presenting basic points on correct throwing to them will allow them to reinforce good form at home.

GOLF BASEBALL

PURPOSE

To develop throwing accuracy and to provide a game to break up practice

EQUIPMENT

A bucket of baseballs, four to six cones

TIME

6 to 8 minutes

PROCEDURE

1. Depending on the number of players, set up four to six cones about 50 feet apart from one another.
2. Divide the team into three groups. Each group throws toward its own cone.
3. Station one coach or parent with each group.
4. Each team's goal is to knock down its cone with the fewest throws possible.
5. The first person in each group throws the ball at the cone. The ball is left where it lands.
6. The second player in each group throws at the cone.
7. As in a foursome in a golf game, the player whose ball is farthest from the cone after the first throw is the first to make the second attempt from where his first throw landed.
8. Again as in golf, each player keeps track of the number of throws it takes to knock over the cone.
9. After each group is finished, the players rotate to the next cone (or hole).

KEY POINTS

Although this game gives the team an enjoyable drill for the players, it still provides players an opportunity to work on throwing skills.

1. Emphasize to the players that they do not have to knock over the cone on a fly. They can knock it over on the bounce.

2. Point out proper throwing technique, such as stepping and following through.

RELATED DRILLS

None

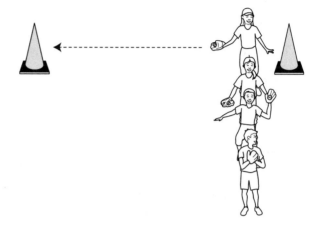

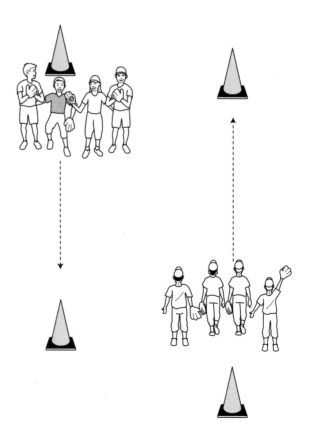

TARGET DRILL

PURPOSE

To improve throwing accuracy for younger players

EQUIPMENT

Soft-covered baseballs, colored masking tape, access to a fence or a wall

TIME

4 to 6 minutes

PROCEDURE

1. On a wall or fence mark off three or four squares with blue painter's tape, 18 inches by 18 inches. The squares should be about 4 to 6 feet apart from each other.
2. Within the large blue squares mark off smaller squares with white tape.
3. Mark a line on the ground in front of each square. The distance between the line and the box depends on the age and skill level of the players.
4. Divide the team into as many groups as there are large squares on the fence or wall.
5. Give each player 3 to 5 balls.
6. The first player in each line throws the ball against the fence.
7. Award one point for throwing the ball within the blue square and two points for hitting one of the smaller white squares.

KEY POINTS

Although it takes a long time to prepare, this is a simple, yet fun and effective, drill for young athletes.

1. In the early stages of the season, emphasize hitting the target as success. With young players, immediate success is important for positive reinforcement and will encourage their enthusiasm for the drill and willingness to listen to instruction.

2. Adjust the distance between the box and the line depending on the age and skill level of the team.

3. Incorporate throwing techniques only after introducing the drill at its elementary level.

Variation

Players can also aim for empty soda cans or plastic cones.

RELATED DRILLS

None

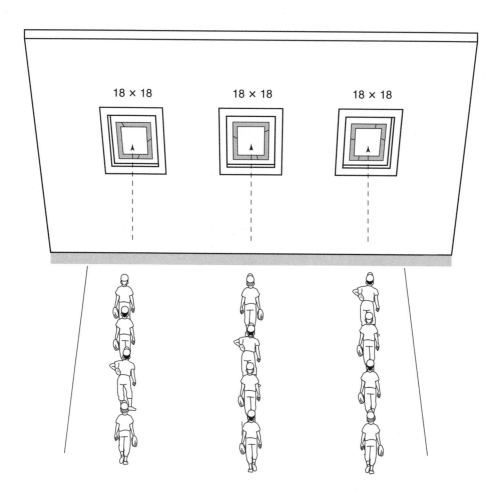

3   # THIRD-BASE DRILL

PURPOSE

To develop the accuracy and strength to make the throw from third base to first base

EQUIPMENT

Four baseballs, gloves

TIME

6 to 10 minutes

PROCEDURE

1. Divide the players into three groups and station them at home plate, third base, and first base. Each player should have a glove.
2. Each group forms a line behind its base.
3. The first person in the line is the first to field the ball.
4. The players behind the fielders are backups.
5. The coach hits a ground ball to the first person in line at third base. The fielder at third base throws it to the fielder at first base. The fielder at first base throws it to the fielder at home plate.
6. After the first person at third base fields the ball and throws to first base, he moves to the end of the line and becomes a backup as the second person in line rotates forward and becomes the fielder.
7. This rotation occurs at each base.
8. After each player goes through the line two or three times, the coach yells, "Rotate." Each group moves clockwise to the next base; the third-base fielders move to first base, and the first-base fielders move to home plate.

KEY POINTS

1. This is a good warm-up drill to use at the beginning of practice. It emphasizes throwing to first base from third base, which is one of the longest and most difficult throws for youth baseball players.

2. This drill works well with two baseballs. As soon as the coach hits the first baseball, the player at home plate tosses the coach a second ball.

3. Keep two extra balls near the coach at home plate; if a ball gets past the fielder at third or first base, the rhythm of the drill will not be interrupted.

4. The coach and the assistant must be safety conscious when two baseballs are being thrown around the infield and as many as 12 players are involved.

5. Because there is a lot of player movement in this drill, spacing is important. The fielders and backups should be evenly spaced apart.

6. Remind players not to hurry their throws.

Variation

In a variation on this drill, called the "bobble drill," the fielder picks up the ball and drops it before making the throw. This teaches players that even if they slightly mishandle a ball, they still have plenty of time to set themselves before making an accurate throw to beat a runner.

RELATED DRILLS

4, 9, 10, 14, 17

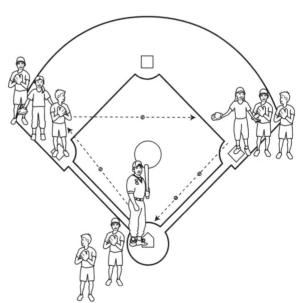

4   LINE THROW

PURPOSE

To develop proper throwing technique, specifically accuracy

EQUIPMENT

One bucket, 20 to 30 hardballs, gloves

TIME

3 to 6 minutes

PROCEDURE

1. Players assemble in two lines, one at the third-base position and the other at the shortstop position.
2. Set up a row of baseballs in front of each line of players.
3. Send two players to first base with an empty bucket. One player is the first baseman and the other is the backup first baseman.
4. On the "go" command, the first person in line at third base runs to the closest ball, picks it up, and throws it to first base. After the throw, the player goes to the end of the shortstop line.
5. The coach gives the "go" command to the first person in the shortstop line, who runs to the closest ball, throws it to first base, then goes to the end of the third-base line.
6. This drill can be done more quickly if the coach gives the "go" command to the next player as soon as the previous player throws the ball.
7. The first baseman receives the throws from the third-base and shortstop positions and places the balls in the bucket. The first baseman rotates with the backup after every five or six throws.

LINE THROW 4

KEY POINTS

1. This drill teaches players to start from the ready position before the pitcher pitches the ball. It also teaches infielders to charge slow rollers and to pick up the balls with their bare hands.

2. When throwing to first base, the fielder must plant the foot and aim between the first baseman's shoulders and abdomen.

3. The first baseman must give the fielders a good target. He keeps his glove open with his arm stretched out at about chest or shoulder height.

RELATED DRILLS

3, 51

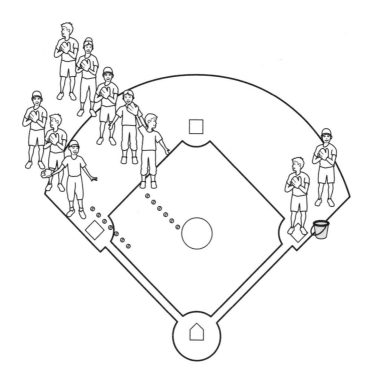

5   LINE MASTER

PURPOSE

To improve hand–eye coordination while forcing players to think ahead

EQUIPMENT

Two soft-covered balls or tennis balls, gloves

TIME

6 to 8 minutes

PROCEDURE

1. All players line up next to each other in a straight line. Make sure there is adequate space between each player.
2. One player steps out 10 to 15 feet from the line and moves to the center, facing the other players.
3. The player facing the line is the "line master" and has one ball.
4. The first person at the end of the line to the line master's right also has a ball.
5. When the coach says, "Go," the line master throws to the second person in line as the first person in line throws the ball to the line master.
6. This drill continues down the line and back again until the two balls return to their original handlers.
7. After one go-round, rotate everyone down the line. The first person in line becomes the line master, and the line master moves to the end of the line.
8. If you have more than 10 players, divide the group into two teams.

KEY POINTS

1. Line master teaches players to think ahead. They must know where the ball is coming from and know ahead of time where they will throw.

2. This drill tests eye–hand coordination. You will see a noticeable difference in the players' reaction times during the course of the year if they practice this drill regularly.

3. Use soft-covered balls, especially if the team is young or it's early in the season.

RELATED DRILLS

17, 19

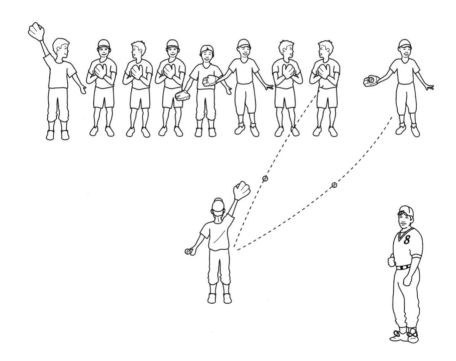

6 RAPID-THROW DRILL

PURPOSE

To develop quickness and proper catching and throwing techniques

EQUIPMENT

One baseball for each pair of players, gloves

TIME

2 to 5 minutes

PROCEDURE

1. Divide the team into pairs. Kids in each pair should be of similar age and skill level.
2. Each pair stands 25 to 30 feet apart, facing each other.
3. For safety purposes, make sure there is at least seven feet between each pair.
4. On the "go" command, partners throw a ball back and forth as fast as they can while keeping their throws under control.
5. After 10, 15, or 20 seconds, the coach yells, "Stop."
6. The players keep track of the number of successful catches they make within the allotted time.
7. Award 10 points for 10 successful catches.
8. After each round, players can move back two or three steps.
9. This game can be played up to any number of points.

KEY POINTS

1. This drill teaches young players how to get the ball out of the glove quickly before throwing. However, you should reinforce the idea that rushing the throw often results in errors and misplays. Players drop balls during this drill if they try to take the ball out of their glove before they have a proper grip.

2. Also emphasize that players must have control of the ball before throwing.

3. The person catching the ball should present a chest-high target for his partner.

RELATED DRILLS

8, 18, 48

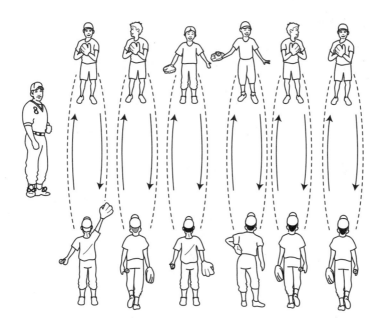

7

PURPOSE

To develop techniques for relaying a baseball from the outfield to the infield

EQUIPMENT

Two buckets of baseballs, six empty plastic buckets, gloves

TIME

10 to 14 minutes

PROCEDURE

1. Divide the players into two teams. Station one team and a coach in right center, and the other team and a coach in left center.
2. Each group has a bucket of hardballs.
3. On home plate, stack six empty plastic buckets into a pyramid.
4. Place one player from each team in the infield.
5. The teams alternate turns.
6. The coach throws the ball high behind the outfielder, preferably hitting the outfield fence.
7. The outfielder turns, locates the ball, runs to it, picks it up, turns, and throws it to the infielder.
8. The infielder pivots after the catch, and throws the ball toward the buckets, trying to knock down as many as possible.
9. The outfielder becomes the infielder, and the infielder goes to the end of the line in the outfield.

KEY POINTS

Emphasize these four points:

1. The infielder waves his hands over his head as the outfielder prepares to throw the ball.
2. The infielder then makes a target for the outfielder with the arms extended at shoulder height.

3. The ball should hit the infielder at shoulder height.

4. The infielder must pivot to the glove side when turning to throw. The term "glove side" is used rather than "right" or "left" because right-handed and left-handed players turn opposite directions before throwing.

Variation

Use a garbage can lying on its side instead of buckets. In this case, the infielder must throw the ball into the garbage can after the relay.

RELATED DRILLS

1, 2, 8

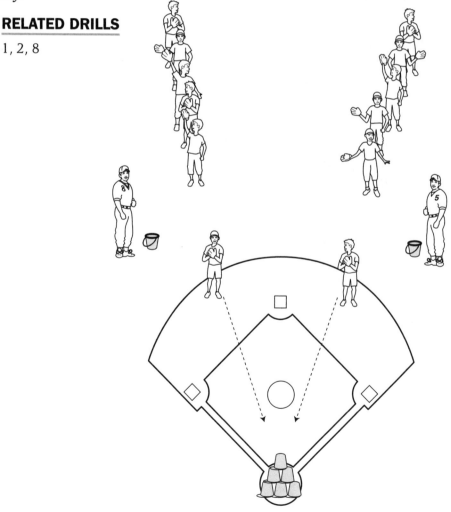

8 THREE-MAN RELAY

PURPOSE

To develop a quick relay from outfielder to infielder

EQUIPMENT

One baseball for each team of three

TIME

5 to 10 minutes

PROCEDURE

1. Divide the team into groups of three.
2. Each group spreads out in a straight line with 15 to 25 yards between each player, depending on the age or skill level of the participants.
3. Place one ball approximately five yards behind the first player in line. On the "go" command, the first player runs, picks up the ball, turns, and throws to the middle player.
4. The middle player catches the ball, turns, and throws to the third player.
5. The third player, after catching the ball, throws it back to the middle player, who then turns and throws the ball back to the first player.
6. The first team to return the ball to the first player receives one point.
7. The first team to seven points wins.

KEY POINTS

This game is similar to the bucket relay.

1. In the three-man relay, the player in the middle receives most of the throws; therefore, it is imperative to rotate players after each round.
2. As the infielder did in the previous drill, the middle player must turn to the glove side when throwing the ball. However, this drill emphasizes getting rid of the ball quickly. Therefore, coaches should remind players to catch the ball cleanly be-

fore attempting to throw it. Younger players will mishandle the ball if they try to throw it before maintaining complete control.

3. Players receiving the ball must give their teammates a shoulder-high target.

Variation

Award points to the team that makes the fewest bad throws or drops the ball the fewest number of times rather than awarding points for quickness.

RELATED DRILLS

1, 2, 17

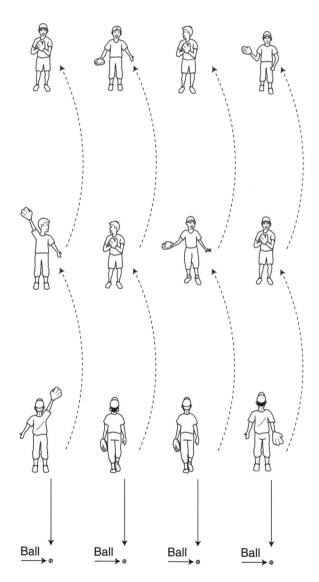

2

Fielding Drills

Fielding skills are vital to the development of young baseball players. Through repetition, players learn to field grounders and catch fly balls and make the play at the base when necessary. Fielding drills teach players proper technique and give them the confidence to put their skills to use at game time.

It is important to emphasize to younger players that when fielding a ground ball in some of these drills, it is just as effective to knock the ball down and keep it in front of the body as it is to catch the ball cleanly in the glove. Catching the baseball with two hands is also a fundamentally sound idea; however, players should not be discouraged from making one-handed catches when the situation calls for it or when it is the only available option.

One of the main mistakes players make when fielding both grounders and fly balls is that they take their eyes off the ball at the last second. Constantly repeating "Watch the ball go into the glove" helps players at almost every age become better fielders.

Coaches should also speak to parents about the appropriate size for a baseball glove. A myth many parents believe is that as their children get older they should buy bigger baseball gloves. Major league infielders, however, wear gloves that are so small that sometimes they seem to be just an outline of the players' hands. Small gloves for an infielder yield much better control because they go exactly where the player's hand goes. Young players sometimes cannot feel or control the entire glove if it is too big. This is especially true when fielding a ground ball backhanded.

These fielding drills can be used as progression-type drills depending on the age and ability of the players involved. Coaches must use their judgment when lengthening or shortening fielding throws in a particular drill. Fielding drills can be performed with two people or in groups. Coaches and parents can create an endless number of drills and variations that are both informative and fun for all youth players.

Using soft-covered balls or tennis balls is an option for younger players early in the season. Keep in mind that these balls, particularly tennis balls, can bounce out of the glove more easily than a regular hardball. The main objective for the young player is to confidently get to the spot the ball is headed to and get a glove on it. Any problem with actually catching the baseball will be overcome with repetition.

A limited variety of fielding drills is always better than a single drill for teaching the basics while maintaining the players' interest. Remember to create challenges and use competition to add fun and increase motivation.

FACE-TO-FACE DRILL

9

PURPOSE

To develop the basic mechanics for fielding a ground ball and following it with an accurate throw

EQUIPMENT

One baseball, gloves

TIME

2 to 4 minutes

PROCEDURE

1. Divide the team into two groups.
2. Line up each group in single-file lines 20 to 30 feet apart, facing each other.
3. The first person in one line throws a grounder to the first person in the other line.
4. After throwing the grounder, the player goes to the end of the line.
5. The person who catches the ball throws a grounder back to the first person in the other line.

KEY POINTS

This is an excellent, fast-paced drill for practicing in an enclosed space.

1. Players should start in the ready position. When in the ready position, players' legs are spread out at shoulder width, their knees are slightly bent, and both hands hang loosely between the knees without touching them. Players should also lean forward a little because it puts weight on the balls of their feet so they are ready to react to any situation.
2. Players should keep their heads down and watch the ball go into their gloves.
3. Each player should step and follow through when throwing a ground ball to the other line.

Variation

Award points for the fewest poor throws. In this situation, teams take turns throwing grounders to the opposing team.

RELATED DRILLS

4, 10, 14, 17

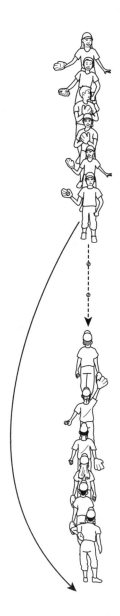

GOALIE DRILL

PURPOSE

To develop positioning and ball-handling skills for keeping a ground ball in front of the body

EQUIPMENT

A bucket of baseballs, gloves, cones

TIME

1 to 2 minutes per person

PROCEDURE

1. Set up two cones 8 to 15 feet apart, depending on the age and ability of players.
2. One player stands between the cones.
3. Another player serves as backup.
4. The coach throws grounders between the cones, and the player tries to stop the ball with his glove before it gets behind him, just as a hockey goalie would sweep away a puck.
5. Award a point for every ball the player stops.
6. Coaches can practice this drill with either a predetermined number of throws to each player or with a time limit.
7. Once done, the fielder moves to the back of the line, the backup becomes the fielder, and the next person in line becomes the backup.

KEY POINTS

This is one of the few drills that teaches players to stop the ball rather than catch it. Learning to knock the ball down while keeping it in front of the body is just as important as catching it with a glove. In game situations many hits are too hard to handle flawlessly; however, with the right mind-set, players can be confident about making the play if they learn to keep the ball in front of them. This drill also emphasizes the importance of keeping the ball in front of the body if it is mishandled or dropped.

1. Players should not try to anticipate which side the coach will throw to.

2. The players can dive toward the baseball if they can do so safely.

3. It is important that players move toward the ball instead of just reaching for the ball with their arms while staying in one place.

4. Because this drill involves two players at a time, try to assemble as many of these stations as you can to keep as many players as possible actively participating. Assistant coaches or even other players can throw the ground balls.

RELATED DRILLS

4, 14, 17

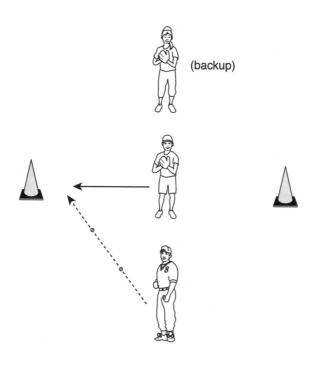

(backup)

11   RACQUETBALL DRILL

PURPOSE

To learn to read a fly ball

EQUIPMENT

A racquetball racket, approximately 10 soft-covered sponge-type balls, gloves

TIME

6 to 8 minutes

PROCEDURE

1. All of the players, who have been assigned numbers, and some of the coaches go to right field.
2. A coach or an assistant coach goes to home plate with a racket and a bucket of soft-covered balls.
3. The coach supervising in the outfield calls out a number.
4. The coach at home plate hits the ball into right field as high as he or she can.
5. The player whose number is called tries to catch the ball.
6. Repeat the drill until each player's number is called.

KEY POINTS

Youth players have a very hard time catching fly balls. This drill, if followed correctly, improves a player's ability to catch fly balls.

1. When catching a fly ball, a fielder's first step is usually back.
2. The fielder must be able to anticipate where the ball will land.
3. The fielder should catch the ball with two hands.
4. Soft-covered balls are difficult to catch because they tend to pop out of players' gloves. Therefore, players should not be discouraged if early in the drill they have trouble squeezing the ball into the glove.

RELATED DRILLS

12, 13

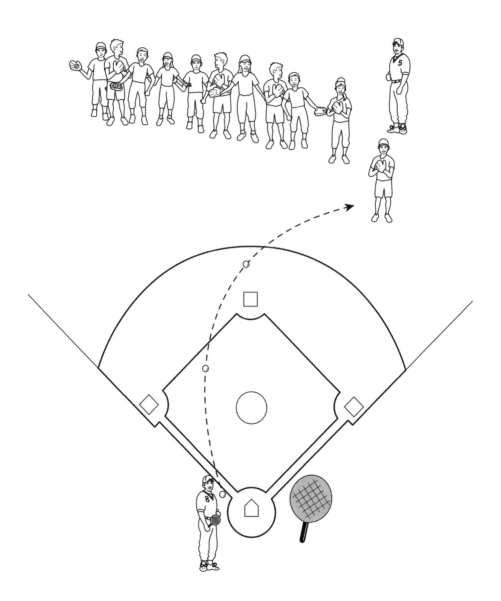

12 VELCRO-BALL DRILL

PURPOSE

To develop confidence in judging the trajectory of a fly ball

EQUIPMENT

One Velcro paddle and ball, a racquetball racket

TIME

4 to 6 minutes

PROCEDURE

1. The coach positions a player about 30 to 40 feet in front of him.
2. The player wears a Velcro paddle in place of a glove.
3. The coach hits the ball high into the air and the player tries to catch it with the paddle.
4. The player throws the ball back to the coach, and another teammate takes a turn.

KEY POINTS

The Velcro paddle and ball reduce a player's fear of catching fly balls.

1. Instruct players to try to catch the ball in front of the head with the arms extended outward.
2. Emphasize that touching or making contact with the ball is as much a success as catching it.
3. Similar to the racquetball drill, the Velcro-ball drill is particularly useful for teaching younger players how to catch fly balls.

RELATED DRILLS

13, 20, 26

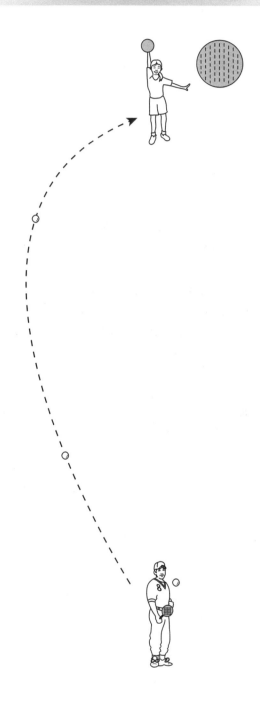

13   LEAD DRILL

PURPOSE

To develop the ability to catch while on the run

EQUIPMENT

A bucket of baseballs, gloves, an empty bucket

TIME

6 to 8 minutes

PROCEDURE

1. The players line up in a single-file line.
2. The coach, with a bucket of baseballs, stands beside the first player.
3. On the "go" command, the player runs away from the coach, looking over his shoulder at the coach.
4. At the opportune time, the coach throws a baseball, "leading" the runner with the throw like a quarterback leading a receiver. The player should not have to break stride to catch the ball.
5. The player catches the ball, drops the ball in the bucket, and returns to the end of the line.

KEY POINTS

This fast-paced drill keeps everyone moving. Players must wait in line only a short time once the drill begins

1. Coaches must teach players to run sideways.
2. Players should never take their eyes off the ball once they locate it in the air.
3. As they run, players should point their lead shoulder in the direction they think the ball will land.
4. Coaches must throw the ball high enough that the players have enough time to judge its projected path.
5. Players should try to make a one-handed catch.

6. Coaches should increase the throwing distances according to the ability of the individual and the team.

7. Turn this drill into a game by counting the number of catches in a row the team can make.

RELATED DRILLS

11, 20, 26

14   SHORT-HOP DRILL

PURPOSE

To develop proper technique for fielding short hops

EQUIPMENT

One baseball per player, gloves, caps

TIME

4 to 6 minutes

PROCEDURE

1. Divide the team into pairs.
2. Players form two lines 10 to 20 feet apart with pairs positioned across from each other.
3. Everyone kneels on two knees. There should be at least five feet between each player in line.
4. When the coach yells, "Throw," the players bounce their balls to their partners, who field them on one hop.
5. Repeat the drill until the predetermined time is up.
6. Next, each player puts his baseball cap approximately three feet in front of him.
7. On the "go" command the players try to hit their partners' baseball caps with the balls.
8. The ball should arrive after one hop.

KEY POINTS

Fielding short hops is one of the most difficult concepts for youth players to master. This drill accustoms players to the short hop. Practicing in the kneeling position forces players to focus on the bouncing ball. In the traditional upright set position, players tend to turn their heads before the ball reaches the glove.

1. Players should keep their eyes on the ball just as they would when practicing catching fly balls.

SHORT-HOP DRILL 14

2. The players must "look the ball" into their gloves.

3. The players should only raise their heads when they feel the baseball securely tucked in the pocket of their glove.

Variation

Two players stand facing each other and take turns throwing short hops to one another. Players earn points for throwing beyond the receiver's reach or for missing the ball. The first player to reach five points loses the game.

RELATED DRILLS

3, 9, 10, 17

15   DIVE-BALL DRILL

PURPOSE

To develop the confidence to leave the feet, or dive, when fielding a hard-hit ball on the ground.

EQUIPMENT

Bucket of baseballs, gloves

TIME

3 to 5 minutes

PROCEDURE

1. Divide the team into two or three groups, depending on the number of available coaches.
2. The coach calls out the first player, who stands 10 to 20 feet from the coach, facing him.
3. The coach takes a ball from the bucket, then yells, "Left." The player moves toward the left, and the coach leads him with the ball so that the player must dive for it.
4. If the player catches the ball, he rolls it back to the coach. Knocking down the ball or stopping it with his body is as good as a catch. The player should kick aside any balls in the active or "diving" area.
5. The coach then yells, "Right." The player moves to his right. The coach leads the player with the ball so that he must dive to catch or stop the ball.
6. Each player gets three or four turns before the next player's turn.

KEY POINTS

The player's main objective is to stop the ball and keep it in front of him instead of worrying about making a spectacular catch.

1. Players should start off in the ready position.
2. Teach players to keep their gloves open as they run to make a backhanded catch.

3. Teach players to run toward the ball to make a catch rather than reaching out and diving for it. A dive should always be a player's last resort.

4. As the players progress, add a player at first base, and instruct the fielders to throw to first after making a diving stop.

Variation

Begin this drill with the players kneeling, diving for the ball from their knees. This variation trains players how to dive even if they aren't in the ready position.

RELATED DRILLS

3, 9, 14, 17

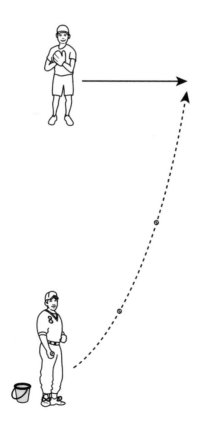

16   BACKHAND DRILL

PURPOSE

To develop the ability to catch a ground ball backhanded

EQUIPMENT

Bucket of baseballs, gloves

TIME

4 to 8 minutes

PROCEDURE

1. Separate the team into two groups and send them to different parts of the field. One coach assists each group.
2. Players in each group line up behind one another.
3. The coach stands approximately 15 feet in front of the players and throws a ground ball to the backhand side of the first player in line. A backhand catch is one in which a player crosses the body with the glove hand to catch the ball, either in the air or on the ground.
4. The fielder starts in the ready position then runs in the direction of the thrown ball, keeping the glove open. After making the catch, the player throws the ball back to the coach, then goes to the end of the other coach's line.
5. Each player in line takes a turn making a backhand catch.

KEY POINTS

This is a progression-type drill. Introduce it early in the season by instructing the players to field the ground balls on their knees.

1. Remind the players to keep their gloves open.
2. Remind players to keep their eyes on the ball at all times.
3. Stopping the baseball and knocking it down can be just as effective as making a clean catch.
4. To ensure that everyone actively participates, set up as many lines for this drill as there are coaches and parents to assist. Players should rotate in and out of the drill quickly.

5. Young players may find catching a baseball backhanded difficult. Make it as easy for them as possible by checking to see if their gloves are properly worked in.

RELATED DRILLS

3, 9, 14, 15, 17

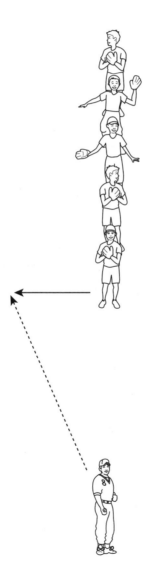

17   CIRCLE DRILL

PURPOSE

To improve concentration when fielding a ball

EQUIPMENT

Several baseballs, gloves

TIME

4 to 6 minutes

PROCEDURE

1. Players form a large circle with plenty of space between them.
2. The coach, standing outside of the circle, throws a ground ball to a player to start the drill.
3. The player catches the ball and then throws a ground ball to any player in the circle except for those very close to him. The next player throws a ground ball to someone else in the circle.
4. After each catch, the coach yells out the number of times in a row the team has caught the ball without errors.
5. The coach then adds a second ball to the drill.

KEY POINTS

1. Players should catch the grounder with two hands and watch the ball go into their gloves.
2. The player should have control of the ball before trying to throw it.
3. To keep more players involved, split the team into two groups with a coach supervising each circle. Set a 30-second time limit and see which circle can catch more grounders without making an error within the allotted time. The winners could earn extra swings during batting practice.
4. Have a few extra balls available to save time in case a player misses a ball.

RELATED DRILLS

3, 9, 14, 15

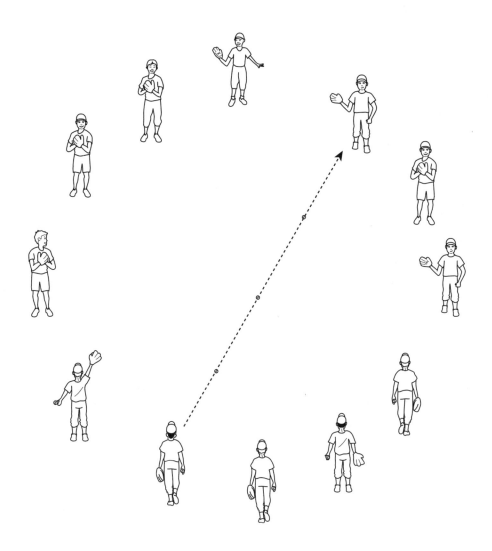

18   REACTION DRILL

PURPOSE

To test and develop a player's reaction time when fielding an on-coming ball

EQUIPMENT

Four tennis balls, gloves, four cones

TIME

4 to 6 minutes

PROCEDURE

1. Place four cones in a square with 10 to 15 feet between cones.
2. The coach stands in the center of the square, and the first player stands next to a corner cone facing away from the coach.
3. The coach throws a tennis ball toward the player, then immediately gives the "go" command.
4. On the "go" command, the player turns and reacts to the ball, trying to make the catch.
5. After catching the ball, the player drops it on the ground next to him.
6. The player runs to the next cone, turns toward the coach, who has already thrown a ball in his direction, and tries to react to the tennis ball in the air before making the catch.
7. When the first player has been to all four cones, it is the next player's turn.

KEY POINTS

1. Players should be ready to catch the ball as they turn around.
2. Players should catch the ball with both hands.
3. Players should concentrate on making sure they catch the ball before running to the next cone.

RELATED DRILLS

14, 22, 24

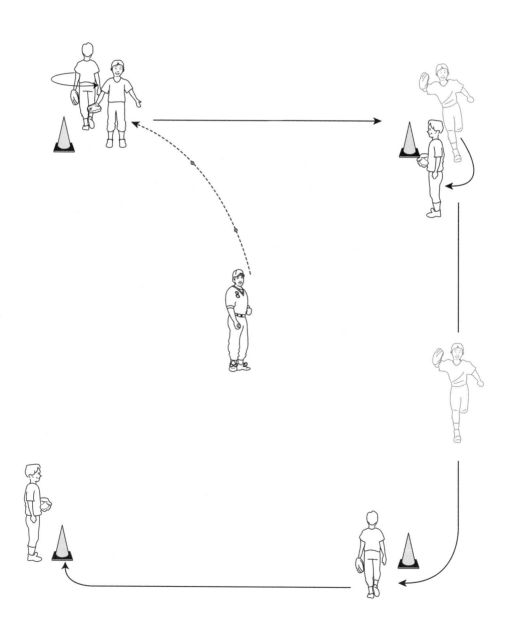

AROUND THE HORN

PURPOSE

To develop accurate and quick fielding skills

EQUIPMENT

A baseball, a stopwatch, gloves

TIME

4 to 8 minutes

PROCEDURE

1. Assign players to third-base, second-base, first-base, catcher, and pitcher positions.
2. On the "go" command the coach starts the stopwatch.
3. The pitcher throws the ball to the catcher, who throws the ball to the third baseman, who throws to the second baseman, who throws back to the first baseman, who finally throws the ball back to the catcher.
4. The coach stops the watch when the catcher receives the ball.
5. A different set of players rotates into the drill.
6. Players should rotate to different positions within the drill.

KEY POINTS

1. This drill works best with five players.
2. Keep a written record of each team's time throughout the season to chart improvements in the drill.
3. Coaches should have extra balls in case of an overthrow.
4. Emphasize that catching the ball smoothly, not the team's time, is the most important aspect of the drill.
5. Players have a tendency to hurry their throws when they are preoccupied with their team's time. Emphasize that hurrying their throws results in errors.

6. Players must step toward the base they are throwing to.

7. The "hot potato" technique (pretending that the ball is hot) teaches players to relinquish control of the ball as soon as possible after the catch.

Variations

1. Place four fielders in a square (the distance depends on the skill level of the four players), and instruct them to throw the ball around the square. As they throw to each other, they should move their feet properly so that the ball is in the center of their bodies as it is caught.

2. Players can throw around the horn once in reverse. To end the drill, the catcher throws the ball to second base as if trying to throw out a runner trying to steal.

RELATED DRILLS

17, 18

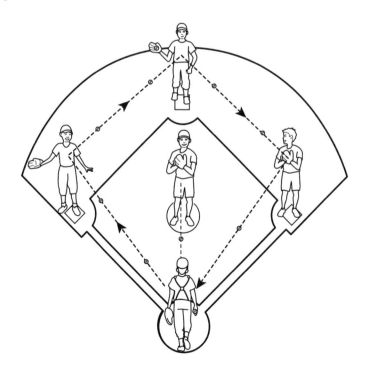

20 OUT-OF-BOUNDS POP FLY

PURPOSE

To develop the technique and confidence to catch a ball near stationary objects such as a dugout or fence

EQUIPMENT

A bucket of baseballs, gloves

TIME

3 to 6 minutes

PROCEDURE

1. Players line up behind one another in foul territory approximately 10 feet from a fence.
2. The coach throws an arcing ball toward the fence.
3. The first player catches the baseball up against the fence, places the ball in the bucket near the coach, then goes to the end of the line.
4. The coach throws to the next player.

KEY POINTS

One of the most difficult things for young players to do is catch a pop fly near an obstacle such as a fence because they fear running into it and getting hurt.

1. Players should extend the free arm or glove arm toward the fence or obstacle and concentrate only on the pop fly. Extending the arm will let the player know when he is close to or making contact with the fence.
2. In this drill catching one handed is fine.
3. If players feel they are getting too close to the fence on a really high pop-up, they should overplay the ball, feel the fence, and then come back to make the play.

4. To keep players on their toes, coaches should throw the pop-up toward the field and away from the fence every once in a while. Therefore, much like in real game situations, players must be able to anticipate the ball coming from any direction and learn to react accordingly.

5. Not all players will be comfortable with this drill. Allow less-experienced players to begin the drill very close to the fence, almost touching it.

RELATED DRILLS

11, 12, 25

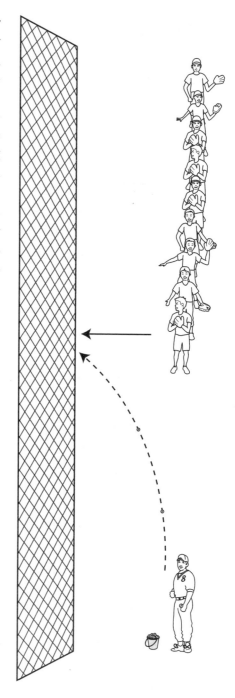

21 FIRST-BASE OVERTHROW

PURPOSE

To practice the procedure for an overthrown ball at first base

EQUIPMENT

A baseball, batting helmet, gloves

TIME

6 to 10 minutes

PROCEDURE

1. Position players at every infield position. They should be in the ready position.
2. Put a base runner at first base.
3. The coach has already placed a baseball, without the fielders knowing where, in foul territory behind first base to simulate an overthrown ball.
4. On the "go" command, the base runner takes off for second base.
5. The first baseman finds the ball, then throws it to the infielder covering second base.

KEY POINTS

This effective team drill teaches players what to do after mishandling the ball.

1. The first baseman must first locate the baseball.
2. The shortstop should cover second base.
3. The second baseman should stay out of the way of the throw. He should direct the first baseman if the first baseman has trouble locating the ball.
4. The first baseman must throw accurately to second to keep from making another overthrow.
5. In this drill, the runner should slide. The shortstop must adjust to the throw to properly tag the sliding runner.
6. The left fielder should back up the infielders at the angle of the incoming ball in case of another overthrow.

RELATED DRILLS

22, 28, 70

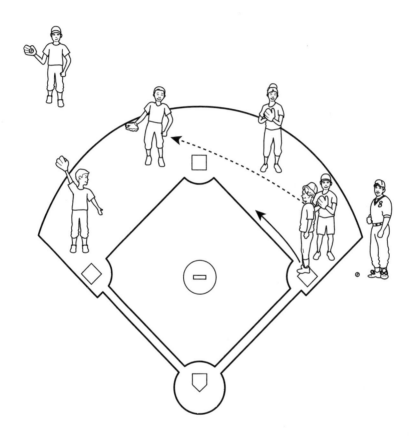

WILD PITCH

PURPOSE

To develop tactics for handling a wild pitch with a runner on third base

EQUIPMENT

A baseball, gloves

TIME

6 to 8 minutes

PROCEDURE

1. Situate the fielding team in their regular positions.
2. Put a base runner on third.
3. The coach places a baseball somewhere behind the catcher without the catcher knowing where.
4. On the "go" command the base runner sprints for home plate.
5. The catcher turns to locate the baseball, and the pitcher runs to cover home plate.
6. When the catcher locates the ball, he turns and tosses it to the pitcher covering home. The pitcher tags the sliding runner with the ball.

KEY POINTS

This situation occurs in almost every youth baseball game and is very rarely practiced. This is an easy drill to set up, and if practiced correctly, can prepare players for real game situations.

1. While running to cover home plate, the pitcher should yell to the catcher where the ball is if the catcher has trouble locating it.
2. The catcher should concentrate only on locating the ball. After doing so, he should turn and toss the ball underhand and low to the pitcher so that the pitcher's glove will be in a good position to tag the sliding base runner.

3. The pitcher should concentrate on catching the ball before turning toward the base runner.

4. Because this is practice, the base runner should, at first, slow up a few feet before reaching home plate so that fielders can effectively practice the drill.

5. When this play occurs, either in practice or in a game, the second baseman should move to the base of the mound to back up the toss to the pitcher. This backup can prevent additional runs if the catcher overthrows the toss to the pitcher and there is more than one runner on base.

6. Rotate all of the pitchers and catchers in this drill.

RELATED DRILLS

21, 28, 70

23   RUN AT BASE RUNNER

PURPOSE

To familiarize fielders with the "two players on one base" game situation

EQUIPMENT

A baseball, gloves

TIME

6 to 8 minutes

PROCEDURE

1. All infielders play in their usual positions except the shortstop. The shortstop plays 15 feet in front of the usual position.

2. Two base runners stand between second and third base, approximately 10 feet from one another.

3. Without the shortstop looking (he shouldn't turn around) the two base runners should locate themselves in an odd, yet common, youth baseball situation such as (1) the one mentioned above or (2) two players on one base. Youth players tend to make all kinds of base running errors that are so unusual that fielders are not sure what to do. This drill teaches the fielders to pursue the lead runner. The coach stands in front of the shortstop and directs both runners. He can direct both back toward second or both toward third. He can tell the lead runner to go to third and the trail runner to go to second. He can also keep base runners where they are.

4. The coach gives the ball to the shortstop and tells him to go after the lead runner.

5. On the "go" command, the shortstop turns around.

6. The base runners break (or stay still) according to the direction given.

7. The shortstop runs at the lead runner and/or throws to the lead base, depending on how close he is to the base runner and how close the base runner is to the lead base. If the short-

stop is close enough to the runner to run him down and tag him, he should do so. However, if the shortstop is unable to catch the runner, then he should throw to the lead base.

KEY POINTS

In the drill, the two base runners serve as a distraction as the fielder faces the "two players on one base" situation.

1. The fielders must always run at the lead runner.
2. Once the lead runner commits to a base, the fielder should try to run him down.
3. If the fielder cannot catch the runner, he should throw to the lead base.
4. Give each infielder a chance to perform this drill as a runner and as a fielder.
5. Teach outfielders to move in when they see this situation so they can serve as a backup.

Variation

This drill has many variations: two players on the same base, two players between first and second, two players between second and third, and two players between third and home.

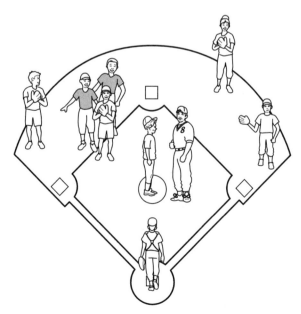

RELATED DRILLS

24, 63

RUNDOWN DRILL

PURPOSE

To rehearse rundown situations for fielders and runners

EQUIPMENT

Three baseballs, four bases, gloves

TIME

3 to 6 minutes

PROCEDURE

1. Divide the team into four groups of three players.
2. Two teams of three sit out.
3. The other two teams head to the field. Each team positions two fielders on one of the base paths (except between home and first). They should stand 15 to 20 feet apart from one another, and one of the players should have a ball.
4. The coach sends a base runner to stand between two of the fielders on one of the base paths.
5. On the "go" command, the base runner attempts either to advance to the next base or return to the base he came from.
6. The fielders throw the ball back and forth to one another as they try to tag the runner out.
7. After the team completes the rundown (which should take no more than 10 seconds), rotate in the teams that sat out. Coaches can also set up mock base paths in other locations away from the field so that every player actively participates at the same time.

KEY POINTS

This drill gives players a good taste of what it is like to be in a rundown. This drill can involve six players at once on the base paths on the field, and the teams that sit out are only inactive for a short time.

1. The fielders should force the base runners back to the base they came from. The infielder who catches the first throw should first walk slowly toward the other fielder to cut down the distance of each subsequent throw. This also decreases the distance that the base runner must run. Cutting the distance is important for youth players because the shorter the throw, the smaller the chance for errors.

2. The fielder should hold the ball at ear level so that the fielding partner can see it.

3. The fielders should not pump the wrist while holding the ball. Although it might fake out the runner, the player might drop the ball on the pump.

4. The fielder should squeeze the ball with the glove when tagging a runner so that the ball does not fall out of the glove.

Variation

The base runner receives one point for making it safely back to the base he came from and two points for advancing to the next base. The fielders receive one point for tagging the runner out before he reaches either base.

RELATED DRILLS

23, 63

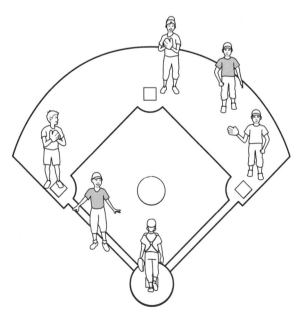

SCREAM DRILL

PURPOSE

To practice calling off another fielder on a fly ball

EQUIPMENT

Bucket of balls, gloves

TIME

4 to 8 minutes

PROCEDURE

1. Place two lines of three players in the outfield, one line in right center and the other in left center, 20 to 30 feet from each other.
2. Divide the rest of the team into two lines 10 to 15 feet from each other in the infield: one at second base and the other at the shortstop position.
3. One coach stands five feet behind second base facing the outfield. Another coach stands five feet behind home plate facing the infield.
4. Each coach tells the first two in each of his line to step up.
5. The coach throws the ball between the two fielders, and the player who is the closest to the ball must scream three times, "I got it," or "Mine."
6. After catching the ball, the player throws it back to the coach.
7. After each player has had a turn, the infield lines and outfield lines should switch with one another.

KEY POINTS

This drill includes a lot of player movement and noise (communication), distractions that players must learn to play with. When two players go after a fly ball, a hierarchy determines which position can call off the other. At the youth level, this must be simplified. Different methods work for different teams.

1. Coaches should make sure that when fielders are finished, they run all the way to the outside of the drill area.

2. The player who is closest to the ball usually has priority.

3. Center fielders always have the right-of-way, even on balls close to the infield.

4. If a ball is hit between an infielder and an outfielder, the outfielder has priority because it is easier to catch a fly ball while running in than while running back.

5. Teach players to block the sun with their gloves if they must look into the sun trying to catch a pop fly.

RELATED DRILLS

11, 12, 26

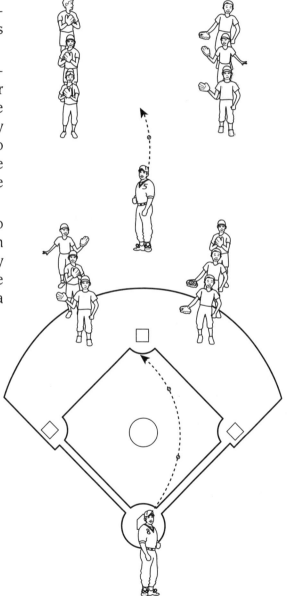

OUTFIELD FLY

PURPOSE

To develop the skills necessary to catch fly balls

EQUIPMENT

Two buckets of baseballs, fungo bat, gloves

TIME

6 to 10 minutes

PROCEDURE

1. Position two infielders, one on either side of second base, a few feet into the outfield grass where they would normally catch a cutoff throw.
2. Set up a line of players in right field and a line of players in left field.
3. One coach stands between home plate and first base. The other coach stands between home plate and third base. Each has a bucket of balls.
4. A parent or coach should monitor both lines in the outfield.
5. A coach, with a fungo bat, hits a fly ball to the first player in the right field line.
6. The player throws the ball into the cutoff man at second base, runs along the outer part of the outfield, and returns to the end of the other outfield line.
7. The other coach hits a fly to the first person in the left field line, who throws the ball into the cutoff man at shortstop. The fielder runs along the outer part of the outfield and returns to the end of the other outfield line.

KEY POINTS

1. The more the coaches or parents are involved with this drill the safer it is for the players.
2. If the ball is angled, fielders should run sideways with their lead shoulder pointing in the direction of the fly ball.

3. If coaches accidentally ground a ball, the players should play it. Outfielders should charge a slow-moving ground ball.

RELATED DRILLS

11, 12, 25

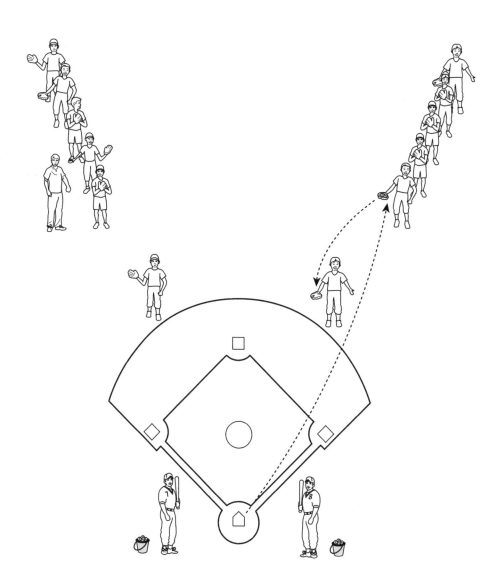

27 INFIELD AND OUTFIELD FULL HOUSE

PURPOSE

To develop fielding skills for infielders and outfielders

EQUIPMENT

Plenty of baseballs, gloves

TIME

6 to 8 minutes or until players become accustomed to the drill

PROCEDURE

1. Set up the infield with players in every position except the catcher and pitcher positions.
2. One coach stands well into foul territory between home plate and third base. Another coach stands well into foul territory between home plate and first base.
3. One or two players stand next to each (preferably two catchers) who will retrieve the balls for them.
4. A third coach stands approximately five feet beyond second base in the outfield. This coach also has a player nearby to catch balls.
5. Three players line up in right field. The remaining players line up in left field.
6. The coach in the outfield hits the ball to the first player in line at right field, who catches the fly ball and throws it to the player near the outfield coach. The right fielder runs to the end of the line in left field.
7. The same coach hits a second ball to the first person in line at left field, who catches the ball and throws it to the player near the outfield coach, then runs to the end of the line in right field.
8. At the same time, the infield coaches hit ground balls to their infielders.
9. The coach on the third-base line alternates hitting balls to the first baseman and the second baseman. The coach on the first-base line alternates hitting balls to the third baseman and the shortstop.

10. After an infielder catches the ball, he throws it back to the player next to the appropriate coach.

KEY POINTS

This is one of the best drills for keeping all the players moving and for allowing the players to practice lots of repetitions.

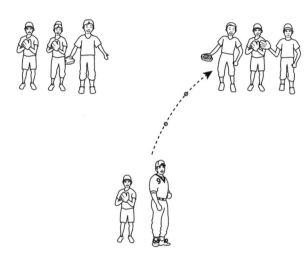

1. Alternate players after a determined amount of time.

2. Throw out a challenge at the end of this drill, such as seeing how many balls the infield and outfield can catch in a row error free.

RELATED DRILLS

11, 12, 25, 26

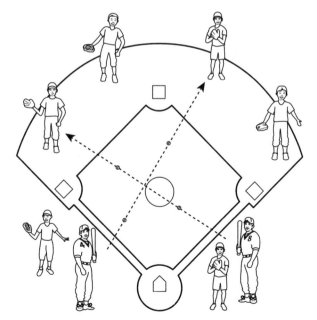

INFIELD OVERHAND OR UNDERHAND THROW

PURPOSE

To teach players at shortstop and second base when to throw the ball overhand and when to toss it underhand.

EQUIPMENT

Bases, gloves, a bucket of baseballs

TIME

6 to 8 minutes

PROCEDURE

1. Place one player at second base.
2. Divide the rest of the players into two lines: one at the shortstop position and one at the second-base position.
3. The coach stands between home plate and the pitcher's mound with a bucket of baseballs and rolls a grounder to the player at shortstop, who throws the ball overhand or tosses it underhand to the player at second base depending on which side the ball is recovered from.
4. The shortstop returns to the end of the second-base line after finishing the play.
5. The player standing at second base catches the throw and rolls the ball underhand back to the coach.
6. After throwing a grounder to the shortstop, the coach immediately throws a grounder to the next second baseman in line.
7. The second baseman must throw the ball overhand or toss it underhand to the player covering second base.
8. The coach can alternate throwing grounders to the right and left side of the fielders.

KEY POINTS

This infield drill gives each player a chance to field the ball to the left and right side. More important, each player must decide whether to throw the ball overhand or to toss it underhand for the out.

INFIELD OVERHAND OR UNDERHAND THROW

28

1. If the shortstop retrieves the ball going toward the right (away from second), he should throw the ball overhand. If he retrieves the ball going toward the left (toward second), he should toss the ball or flip it underhand so that the player at second base can easily handle it.

2. If the second baseman retrieves the ball going toward the left (away from second), he should throw the ball overhand. If he retrieves the ball going toward the right (toward second), he should toss the ball or flip it underhand so that the short-stop at second base can easily handle it.

3. The fielder must maintain control when flipping the baseball underhand. If the flip is too high, the run-ner has a chance to beat the throw.

4. When fielding the ball away from sec-ond base, the player must pivot, hop, or skip his body to face the base he's throw-ing to.

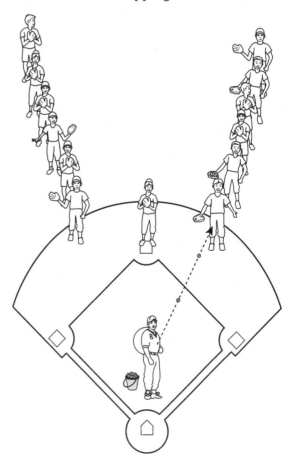

Variation

Conducting this drill with two coaches and two players on each side of second base increases the speed of the drill and allows the players more repetitions.

RELATED DRILL

70

63

29 DESPERATION THROW

PURPOSE

To develop catching, fielding, and immediate throwing skills during a last-ditch effort for the final out at home plate.

EQUIPMENT

A bucket of baseballs, gloves

TIME

4 to 6 minutes

PROCEDURE

1. Position two catchers at home plate in full gear.
2. Divide the rest of the players into the three outfield positions.
3. The coach stands near the pitcher's mound with a bucket of baseballs and simulates a hit by throwing a ball to one of the outfield positions.
4. The first player in line charges the ball, picks it up, and throws it home, all in one fluid motion.
5. The catcher gets into position to catch the ball and tag the runner out.
6. The coach throws to each outfield position in turn.
7. The two catchers rotate after three or four throws.

KEY POINTS

This game situation usually appears sometime during the course of a season, but teams rarely practice it. Every player should practice this drill.

1. Explain the do-or-die situation to the players. For example, their opponent may have the winning run at second base, and with a hit into the gap, the runner could try to score if you don't make the out at home.
2. This drill is also effective at guarding against a runner tagging up at third with fewer than two outs.

3. Players should watch the ball go into their gloves before lifting their heads to throw the ball home.

RELATED DRILL

26

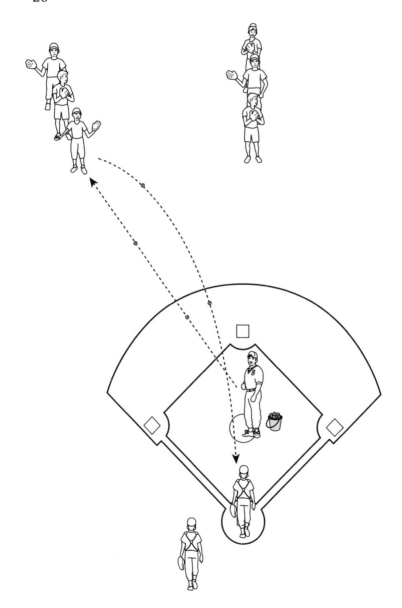

3

Hitting Drills

Hitting is the most popular exercise for youth players in baseball practices and games. However, because your goal for practice is to keep as many players actively involved at one time as possible, avoid running an old-fashioned batting practice: one player taking 10 to 15 swings while the other players watch from the field in boredom. This wastes valuable time. Instead, use parents or assistant coaches to set up one or two stations for warm-ups such as hitting off a tee or taking soft tosses. This keeps the other players involved as they wait their turn for regular batting practice.

The popularity of the batting tee has made batting drills more effective. Batting tees come in many types and in a range of prices; however, the simplest batting tee is fine for youth players. The most common hitting mistakes youth players make are uppercutting the ball, taking too big a front step or stepping toward third base (for a right-hander) instead of toward the pitcher, and taking an incomplete swing. Practicing off a tee, which is the best way to teach youngsters to swing "high to low," can correct many of these mistakes. Coaches must emphasize that any contact off the tee is good and that players should not be preoccupied with how far they can hit the ball.

The toss drill, with its endless variations, is another great way for young players to improve their hitting, and they can perform a toss drill with a teammate instead of relying on a coach. In many toss drills the coach or partner tosses a ball and the player hits it into a net or screen. However, a safer alternative is to make a "rag ball." Wrap a couple of rags together into a ball and secure it with one- or two-inch-wide masking tape. Be sure not to wrap the tape too tightly. This will avert dangerous "bounce backs" when the rag ball is hit off of a wall.

Bunting is a skill that is underused and underpracticed in youth baseball. The two techniques that are advocated are the square bunt and the pivot bunt. The square bunt begins as the pitcher's front foot comes down to the ground during the windup. The batter moves the front foot back and the back foot forward so that the two feet are even with and parallel to one another. In other words, the player's shoulders and feet are square to the pitcher. On the other hand, during the pivot bunt, the player does not move the feet but instead pivots on the front of both feet at the end of the pitcher's windup. The shoulders in this technique are also square to the pitcher. The pivot bunt is preferred because in the square bunt, the player can inadvertently step on home plate or out of the batter's box when lifting both feet and replanting them.

In both bunting techniques, the player should hold the bat softly, not squeezing it too tightly. The top hand should move up on the bat only six to eight inches; young players tend to move the top hand too high. Players should hold the bat with the thumb, index finger, and middle finger of the upper hand, but to protect the fingers they should not wrap them around the bat. As the ball comes toward home plate, the fat part of the bat (the barrel) should be higher than the handle. If the handle is higher during a bunt, the ball will usually go foul or pop up. During the bunt, the batter should try to catch the ball with the bat. The player can picture a pane of glass behind him that he must protect by catching the ball with the bat. Players should try to hit toward third base, which means a longer throw. The ball should bounce once or twice on the dirt and then slow up on the grass.

Choosing an appropriate bat can be confusing. Parents tend to pay too much for a bat that the player will grow out of in a year or two. Coaches should encourage players not to fall in love with just one bat. Trying different bats in practice is a great way for kids to learn to hit with a degree of flexibility.

BUBBLE BASEBALL

PURPOSE

To develop different stages of hitting, particularly hand–eye coordination

EQUIPMENT

One or more large plastic bats, one or more bottles for blowing bubbles

TIME

4 to 6 minutes depending on whether the drill is performed with a team or individually

PROCEDURE

1. The player holds a plastic bat; the grip is not important.
2. A coach or a parent kneels in front of the player and blows bubbles out of a bottle.
3. The player swings the bat at the floating bubbles.

KEY POINTS

This most basic drill is not only incredibly fun for young players, it also teaches the difficult skill of hitting a moving target.

1. Kids as young a three can perform this drill; however, all age groups can benefit from hitting an unpredictable moving target.
2. The player does not remain stationary or in the batter's box but instead chases the moving bubbles around the field or backyard.
3. This drill is more appropriate for one-on-one practice than for team practice.
4. Do not stress technique. Successfully hitting the bubbles is the most important goal for this drill.

RELATED DRILLS

None

31 BEACH BALL TEE BALL

PURPOSE

To teach players how to hit off a batting tee

EQUIPMENT

Batting tees, a bathroom plunger, a bat, beach balls

TIME

6 to 8 minutes, or individual instruction

PROCEDURE

1. Place a batting tee at home plate.
2. Stick a bathroom plunger into the tee with the rubber part facing up.
3. Place a beach ball or a large lightweight ball on top of the plunger.
4. The player stands next to the batting tee and hits the ball off the plunger with the bat.
5. Each player can take three or four swings.

KEY POINTS

Hitting a baseball is one of the hardest skills in sports to master; however, this low-skill drill for very young baseball players offers a guarantee of success.

1. In this particular drill, the less instruction you attempt the better. Limit comments to nothing more than "Hit the beach ball" and "Watch the bat hit the ball."
2. Younger players have a tendency to turn their heads before the bat strikes the ball. If a player has this problem, start him out with a quarter or half swing before striking the ball.
3. A top-of-the-line batting tee is not necessary for younger players; a tee that supports a large ball is sufficient.
4. Set up several stations to keep all players actively involved.

5. This is an excellent parent–child drill that can and should be practiced in the backyard. This drill works well against a net, a tarp, and even the side of a house or apartment building.

6. Teams and individuals can progress to smaller and smaller balls over a period of weeks or even days.

RELATED DRILLS

None

32   BAT-SIZE DRILL

PURPOSE

To choose proper bat size and weight so that the batter can hit comfortably

EQUIPMENT

A selection of bats in various sizes and weights

TIME

30 seconds

PROCEDURE

1. The player selects the bat that he wants to hit with and holds it by the knob with the arm extended. The arm is extended in front of the player with the bat horizontal to the ground.

2. If the player can hold the position for 30 seconds, the bat size is OK. If he cannot, the bat might be too heavy. If the bat starts to drop or even shake a little in the player's extended hand, the player should choose a lighter bat.

KEY POINTS

Bat selection is important for baseball players of all ages, especially younger ones, because they tend to use bats that are heavier than necessary.

1. Smaller players should use lighter bats for a quicker swing.

2. Lighter bats also increase bat control.

3. Parents should evaluate different bat sizes and weights for their kids before spending a fortune. Sometimes a $30 bat is just as effective as a $200 bat.

4. Coaches should emphasize the importance of being flexible in bat choice rather than falling in love with a particular bat.

5. A second technique for selecting a bat is for the player to hold out one hand horizontally. With the other hand, he holds the bat near the end of the handle with the bat resting against his side. The player raises the bat into the same horizontal position as the free hand, without bending the elbow, and holds it for 30 seconds. Not being able to hold up the bat usually means that the bat is too heavy. The coach should recommend a lighter bat.

RELATED DRILLS

None

33 OVERCOMING BATTER'S FEAR
DRILL 1

PURPOSE

To alleviate a player's fear of getting hit by a pitch

EQUIPMENT

Soft-covered balls, a bat

TIME

Approximately 10 minutes or until each player has a turn

PROCEDURE

1. The coach pitches a soft-covered ball to a batter with the intent to hit him.
2. When the pitch reaches the batter's body, the batter turns into the pitch so that the ball hits his back.

KEY POINTS

The fear of getting hit by the ball is a common problem for youth players and hinders their hitting ability.

1. Turning in so that a tennis or soft-covered ball hits the player in the back may alleviate his fear of being hit in a game.
2. A player who greatly fears being hit should use a pivot bunt instead of a square bunt. Bunting successfully builds a player's confidence in the batter's box.

RELATED DRILLS

34, 35

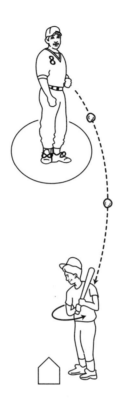

34 OVERCOMING BATTER'S FEAR DRILL 2

PURPOSE

To alleviate a player's fear of getting hit by a pitch

EQUIPMENT

Access to a chain link fence, a bat, a soft-covered ball

TIME

5 to 10 minutes

PROCEDURE

1. A pitcher or coach stands on one side of a fence.
2. A batter stands on the other side of the fence facing the pitcher.
3. The distance between the pitcher and batter should be an approximate Little League pitching distance of 45 feet.
4. The pitcher throws a soft-covered ball into the fence.
5. The batter either swings the bat, or he moves away from the oncoming pitch if he thinks the ball would hit him if there were no fence.

KEY POINTS

This is an effective method for alleviating a young batter's fear of an oncoming ball. Although we teach players to turn into the ball, they can also bail out of the batter's box. The point of these drills is to teach the players to handle the indecisive moment when they might "freeze" at an inside pitch. By repeating this drill, the batter can learn to decide earlier whether to turn or bail.

1. If the ball looks like a strike, the batter should swing.
2. If the ball comes right at the batter, he should turn into the ball so that, if the fence were not there, the ball would hit him in the back or on the helmet. The proper helmet will protect the player's head and ear. A proper helmet should fit comfortably on a player's head. It should also be a little snug over the player's ears. You do not want the helmet too loose because

if it does fall off when the player is running the bases, he can be in harm's way of a thrown ball.

3. The coach should throw strikes and wild pitches to keep the batter on his toes.

RELATED DRILLS

33, 35

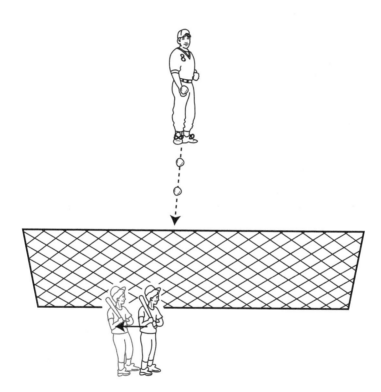

35 OVERCOMING BATTER'S FEAR DRILL 3

PURPOSE

To alleviate a player's fear of getting hit by a pitch and to teach a player to keep the back foot planted while batting

EQUIPMENT

One or two wooden two-by-fours approximately 36 inches long, a soft-covered ball, a bat

TIME

5 to 10 minutes or until each player has a turn

PROCEDURE

1. A player takes a natural stance in the batter's box
2. Place the two-by-four against the back of the batter's back foot.
3. Pitch a soft-covered ball toward the batter.
4. If the ball is a strike, the player should swing the bat. If the ball looks like it might hit the batter, the batter should turn the front shoulder in toward the catcher so that the ball hits him squarely in the back.

KEY POINTS

Teaching players how to deal with the potential of being hit by a pitch is important. Many youth players are wary of being plunked by the baseball, and it affects their stance and hitting. Players afraid of being hit tend to lift the back leg and move the back foot, which should only move during the natural twisting motion of swinging a bat. When the back foot moves, it might wander in the batter's box and affect the batter's stance and chances of hitting the baseball.

1. The wood against the back foot limits foot movement and makes the player aware that the foot must remain planted.
2. Using two pieces of wood, one on each side of the foot, further limits the foot's movement. One or two bricks could also be used.

3. Remind the batter that the front foot must step toward the pitcher six to eight inches on every pitch. The back foot, however, remains stationary except for the minor twisting experienced when swinging the bat.

4. The stance itself can either help or hinder the player's efforts to move away from the ball. Too much weight on the front foot hinders the player's ability to move out of the ball's way. The proper stance and a six-inch step toward the pitcher with the front foot keep the batter balanced, which makes it easier to move out of the way.

RELATED DRILLS

33, 34

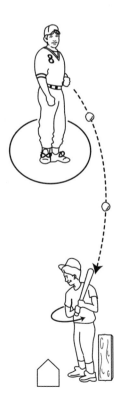

TOSS DRILL

PURPOSE

To develop hitting accuracy and technique through repetition

EQUIPMENT

A bat, a bucket of soft-covered balls or rag balls, access to a fence

TIME

2 to 4 minutes per player

PROCEDURE

1. One player with a bat faces a fence three to five feet away.
2. The coach kneels next to the player on a 45-degree angle
3. The coach tosses the ball underhand in front of the batter. The player swings at the ball and hits it against the fence.
4. The player gathers the balls and puts them in a bucket for the player in the next round.

KEY POINTS

This is one of the most effective hitting drills because players are guaranteed a lot of swings in a short time.

1. Use soft-covered balls or rag balls that won't bounce forcefully off the fence toward the player. Besides being safer, softer balls won't damage the fence.
2. The player should practice a level swing rather than taking an uppercut at the ball. The ball should hit the wall or fence no higher than the batter's shoulder height.
3. Eventually players can pair up for this drill. One player can toss to the hitter, then the players can switch positions.
4. Safety is a major concern. Make sure there is plenty of space between hitters and that all batters begin their turn at the same time. No one should gather the balls until everyone is finished.
5. Younger players can use a big plastic bat for this drill.

6. To discourage players from turning their heads too soon when swinging, instruct them to yell, "Hit" when the bat makes contact with the ball.

Variations

1. High and low. This drill is a challenge for youth players. The coach tosses two rag balls from one hand and calls out either "High" or "Low." The batter must swing at whichever ball the coach calls out.

2. Color ball. The coach has six rag balls. Three are wrapped in white masking tape; three are wrapped in blue painter's tape. Instead of calling out, "High," or "Low," he calls out, "White," or "Blue," and the player swings at whichever ball the coach calls out.

3. Bunting. Using rag balls for bunting is an easy and effective variation. A player tosses the rag ball to a partner in the bunting position, who bunts the ball into the fence. More advanced players can use a broom handle instead of a bat.

RELATED DRILL

38

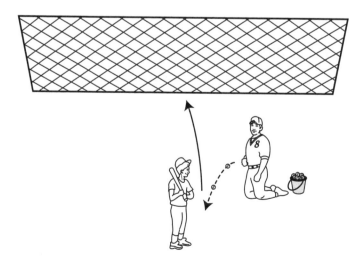

37   TEE-BALL DRILL

PURPOSE

To develop hitting technique and teach batters to keep their eyes on the ball when swinging

EQUIPMENT

A batting tee, a ball, a bat

TIME

4 to 6 minutes per player

PROCEDURE

There are hundreds of variations for hitting drills off of a batting tee. This is the procedure for the most basic drill.

1. The player gets into his stance next to a batting tee located in front of a fence, net, or tarp.
2. The coach places a hardball or soft-covered ball on the batting tee.
3. The player swings at the ball and returns to his stance.
4. The coach puts another ball on the tee.

KEY POINTS

Baseball players at every level recognize the importance of the batting tee as a powerful instructional tool. Some major league players hit 50 to 100 balls off a tee before practice or a game.

1. Players should keep their eyes focused on the ball and watch it leave the tee during the swing. Younger players have a tendency to turn their heads at the last second before the bat strikes the ball. Hitting the top of the tee instead of the center of the ball is one indication that this is happening.
2. If a player turns his head as he swings, instruct him to yell, "Hit" as the bat contacts the ball. This forces the player to watch the ball as the bat makes contact with it.
3. If the player still has trouble with this drill, use a larger ball such as a softball.

4. The player can also swing with just the top hand to cure the head turn. If the bat is too heavy to hold with one hand, the player can use a broomstick and a soft-covered ball.

5. Encourage the batter to swing at nothing higher than the shoulders to avoid swinging with an uppercut.

6. Do not practice this drill with a hardball against a metal fence; the ball might bounce back and injure someone. A net or a tarp is the best option for this drill.

7. Players should use bats other than their own to get different feels for hitting the baseball.

RELATED DRILL

39

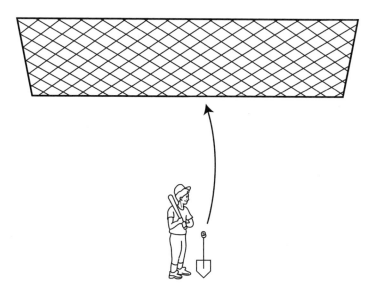

38   CHAIR DRILL

PURPOSE

To develop proper swinging technique, while avoiding an uppercut swing

EQUIPMENT

One batting tee, one chair, a ball

TIME

4 minutes

PROCEDURE

1. Place a batting tee on home plate or in front of a net.
2. Place the chair directly behind the tee with the seat facing the tee.
3. Adjust the tee so that it is slightly lower than the back of the chair.
4. The player swings at the ball on the tee without hitting the chair. The chair acts as a blueprint for how the player's swing should be.

KEY POINTS

This drill corrects a youth baseball player's uppercut.

1. The player should swing with a high-to-low stroke.
2. Hitting the back of the chair indicates an uppercut.
3. This drill is great for individual instruction and can be practiced as little or as much as needed.
4. A player might feel a sting when hitting the chair. Therefore, start younger players off with a plastic bat and ball before progressing to a hardball and bat.

RELATED DRILL

37

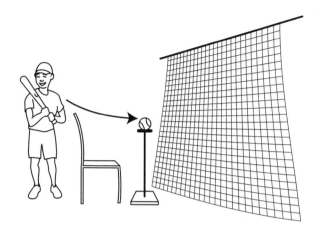

CINDER-BLOCK DRILL

PURPOSE

To develop the eye–hand coordination necessary to hit a moving target

EQUIPMENT

One cinder block; a bucket of baseballs, soft-covered balls, or tennis balls; a net or a tarp

TIME

4 to 8 minutes or five hits per player

PROCEDURE

1. Put a cinder block on the ground 8 to 12 feet in front of a net or a tarp.
2. The batter stands next to the cinder block as if it were home plate.
3. The coach bounces a ball onto the cinder block.
4. The player hits the ball into the net off the bounce.
5. Players rotate in and out of this drill after a predetermined number of hits.

KEY POINTS

This is an excellent fast-paced hitting drill that gives players numerous batting repetitions in a short time.

1. Move away from the batter after bouncing the ball on the cinder block to avoid getting hit.
2. Like in the toss drill, the batter should strike the ball into the net or wall below shoulder height. If the ball hits the wall higher than shoulder height, the batter is uppercutting at the ball.
3. Younger players can use thick plastic bats to hit tennis balls.

4. Don't hit a hardball into a chain-link fence. A hardball can hit the supporting crosspiece and bounce directly back at the hitter.

Variations

1. Batters can also hit the bouncing ball into the field. Fielders can play the ball as if it were a game situation.

2. Younger players can use a tennis racket instead of a bat. This is a popular variation for younger players because it makes the ball easier to hit.

RELATED DRILLS

37, 38

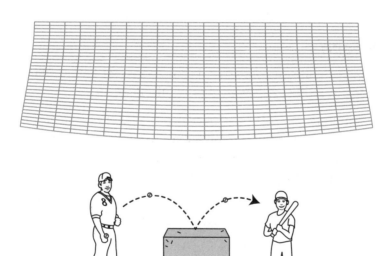

BROOM-HANDLE BUNT

PURPOSE

To develop bunting techniques

EQUIPMENT

One broom handle, a bucket of rag balls or tennis balls

TIME

3 to 5 minutes per player

PROCEDURE

1. A player stands in the batter's box, and the coach stands approximately halfway between the pitcher's mound and home plate.
2. The coach throws or tosses a rag ball underhand to the batter.
3. The batter squares around and bunts the ball.

KEY POINTS

Bunting is a difficult, yet crucial, skill to master and is an important strategy in almost every level of youth baseball.

1. Emphasize that it is not necessary to bunt the rag ball to a particular side of the infield but that making contact with the broom handle is most important.
2. Timing is important when bunting.
3. In this drill, the objective for the batter is to make contact with the ball; therefore, the batter can start in the bunting position.
4. To keep more players actively involved, perform this drill with two or three players.
5. A broom handle is much narrower then a bat, which makes hitting the ball more challenging.
6. When bunting, the batter should not push the bat (or broom handle) into the ball but instead let the ball meet the bat. Batters can imagine that there is a pane of glass right in front of the bat, and if they push the bat forward to bunt the ball they will break the glass.

7. The bat (or broom handle) should be level when in the bunting position. However, the fat end of the bat can be tilted up at a slight angle. If the fat end of the bat is lower than the rest of the bat, the ball will pop up.

RELATED DRILLS

41, 42

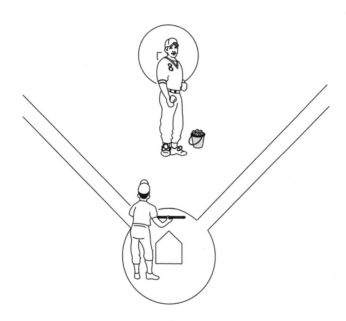

41 GLOVE BUNT

PURPOSE

To develop bunting technique

EQUIPMENT

An old baseball glove, an old bat, a bucket of hardballs

TIME

4 to 6 minutes per player

PROCEDURE

1. Put the barrel of an old bat through the opening in the back of an old glove.
2. Attach the glove onto the bat four to six inches from the end of the bat so that the pocket of the glove is open wide. You can use rope, duct tape, or Velcro.
3. The coach pitches the baseball to the batter.
4. The batter gets into the bunting position.
5. When the ball reaches the batter, he pulls the bat back a few inches and catches the ball in the glove attached to the end of the bat.
6. The coach continues pitching the baseballs in the bucket.

KEY POINTS

This fun backyard baseball drill is an excellent way to teach what coaches call the "soft bunting technique."

1. Securing the glove at the end of the bat might prove somewhat difficult.
2. This is a dual-purpose drill: The glove shows the player where the bat should hit the ball, and it reinforces the idea that bunting is not pushing the bat forward but letting the ball meet the bat. Catching the ball in the glove teaches this soft contact.
3. The fat part of the bat should be held slightly higher than the handle of the bat.

RELATED DRILLS

42, 43

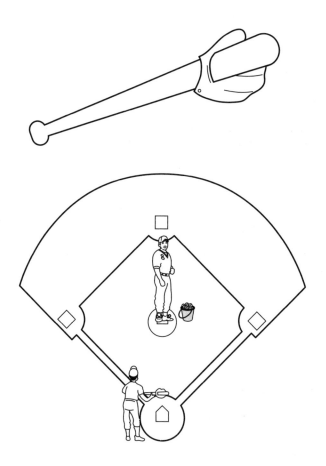

42 BUNT-DRILL BATTING PRACTICE

PURPOSE

To improve bunting technique

EQUIPMENT

Three cones, batting helmets, gloves, balls, bats

TIME

1 minute per player, with two to four pitches each

PROCEDURE

1. Set up three cones on the third-base line about 10 feet from home plate. Place one cone on the line and the others two feet and four feet on the fair side of it.
2. The coach pitches the ball.
3. The batter squares to bunt, trying to bunt the ball between the two outside cones.
4. Award one extra swing during regular batting practice if the batter bunts the ball between the two outside cones.
5. The batter earns two extra swings for knocking down the middle cone.

KEY POINTS

This drill is an excellent motivator for perfecting bunting skills, and it should usually precede batting practice.

1. The batters should assume their regular stance and square to bunt just as the pitcher's front foot is about to hit the ground.
2. The pivot bunt is preferred for younger players. They should pivot on the front of their feet as they square to bunt.
3. The barrel of the bat should be even with or higher than the handle.
4. The hitter should bunt the ball onto the dirt right in front of home plate so that the ball "dies" exactly between the catcher and third baseman.

5. The coach can widen the cones depending on the age of the players or the team's skill. Positive reinforcement is important in this drill.

Variation

Put an object, such as a cone, extra glove, or bucket, five to six feet from the foul line; the coach pitches to the hitter, who tries to "drag bunt" the ball between the foul line and the object. Award five points if the player is successful; deduct five points if the ball reaches the mound. If the ball goes foul, no points are subtracted or added. This encourages the batter to bunt the ball either perfectly or foul.

RELATED DRILL

41

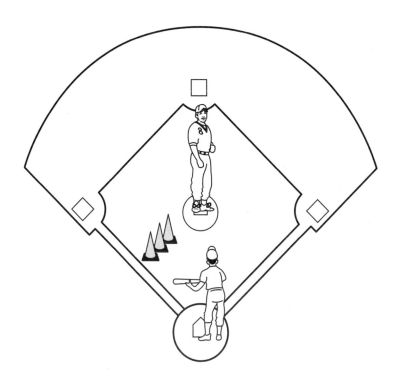

PURPOSE

To develop a batter's concentration during the pitcher's release

EQUIPMENT

Six baseballs, each with a small mark the size of a quarter on two or more sides of the ball; two of the balls should be marked with one color, and the other four with a different color; the colors should be bright and easy to see

TIME

4 to 6 minutes

PROCEDURE

1. The first batter stands in the batter's box.
2. The pitcher takes one of the six baseballs, hiding the colored dot from the batter, and pitches the ball.
3. The batter strides but does not swing and instead calls out the color on the baseball after it is in the catcher's glove.

KEY POINTS

This drill is more appropriate for older players; however, younger players may enjoy the challenge. This drill teaches players to keep their eye on the ball.

1. Starting in a proper stance, the batter prepares as usual and does everything except swing.
2. The batter must follow the flight of the ball and watch it go into the catcher's glove.
3. This drill can be set up as a competition to see which batter can identify the most colors correctly.
4. Divide the team into groups and use assistant coaches to set up two or three stations at one time.
5. Coaches should also throw in a ball without any color to see how players react. Some will guess a color; others will tell the coach they followed the ball but didn't see any color.

RELATED DRILLS

37, 48

PURPOSE

To teach players how to make contact. This drill also stresses the importance of hitting ground balls.

EQUIPMENT

Batting equipment, gloves

TIME

10 to 15 minutes

PROCEDURE

1. Number the players from 1 to 12, assuming that there are 12 players at the practice.
2. Player 1 bats, player 2 is on deck, player 3 is on double deck, and player 4 waits in the dugout. The other players take positions on the field.
3. The coach pitches from in front of the mound.
4. The first batter gets up and stays up for five swings as long as he hits the ball fair and on the ground. The batter is out if he misses the ball, hits it foul, or hits it in the air so that it is caught on a fly.
5. After the first batter is out or has five good swings, the on-deck hitter is up. Player 1 gets his glove and goes into the field.
6. The players rotate up, and player 5 comes in from the field and waits in the dugout.
7. The players who made five good swings can have a playoff or get an additional swing at the next batting practice.

KEY POINTS

Players do not always recognize the situations in which they should shorten their swing. Therefore, practicing this drill regularly can have an incredible impact on a player facing two strikes in a game. In this case, you just have to yell out, "Continuation drill," and the player knows to shorten his swing, which increases bat control. This is a popular and fast-moving drill, and the coach must constantly be aware of the players' safety.

1. Players should hustle in and out of the field.

2. Players must be in their positions, and the on-deck batters must be in safe locations before the coach pitches.

3. Players should not chop down on the ball to force a ground ball. Compacting the normal swing will suffice.

4. Each player should bat at least twice so that those who made outs in their first attempt will have another chance.

Variation

Coaches can divide the team in half. The first team goes through the lineup once before switching sides. Award one point each time a player swings successfully five times.

RELATED DRILLS

75, 78, 79

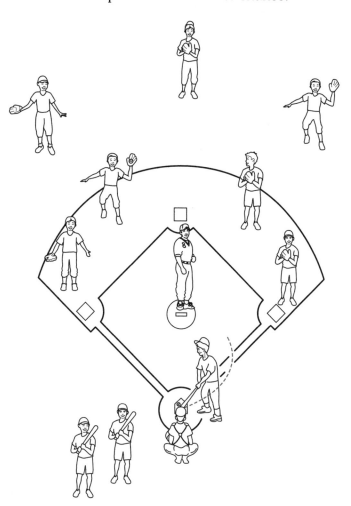

4

Pitching Drills

Pitching is the most dissected and analyzed aspect of youth baseball. Many parents and coaches secure private pitching lessons for their players and send videos of their players pitching for a comprehensive critique of their technique. Although these programs work, the youth parent–coach must also concentrate on certain aspects of pitching during hands-on practice; this could be the only valuable pitching advice some youth players get. One important step a coach can take is to organize team practices several weeks before the season begins. This allows the pitcher time to safely develop arm strength. To improve accuracy and learn to hit the strike zone, beginning pitchers should move closer to home plate and throw into a target, such as a batting net.

Major league pitching coaches use long toss (see drill 47) as a warm-up and to strengthen a pitcher's arm. Youth coaches can learn from the pros and incorporate this drill into their practices. When youth pitchers practice this drill, it is important that as they increase their throwing distance, they don't overthrow the ball just so that it reaches their partners on a fly. If the ball gets to the partner on 1 or 2 bounces, that's fine.

Pitchers should practice a variety of drills that isolate the specific parts of the body that create the pitching motion. The starting position of the pitching motion begins with the player's feet approximately shoulder length apart. The player then begins his windup. If he is a righty, he will move his left foot (lefties move their right foot) back behind the pitching rubber. As he moves his foot back, the pitcher will also swing both arms up from his waist to above his head. The player will then bring his arms down, and as he does, he will pivot on the rubber so he is now facing sideways. He will then bring up his front leg to waist height, then step forward with his front foot. His front foot now faces the batter as he steps. As he plants his front foot, he will throw the ball and subsequently follow through with his entire body, ending up square to the batter's box. Youth pitchers commonly take too big an initial step back, which can throw off the pitching motion. This step should be just six inches. Players must also remember to bend the knees to begin this motion and to raise the front leg as high or higher than the waist. On the follow-through, the player must rotate the hips and end with the throwing arm at the outside of the opposite knee.

Although it is important for pitchers to practice specific drills, youth coaches must fight the tendency to overcoach their pitchers.

Many coaches limit the number of innings a pitcher can pitch during a game. Setting a pitch count limit makes more sense and is becoming more popular.

The use of curve balls in youth baseball has always been a controversial topic. The mechanics involved in throwing a curve can affect the developing arm of a young player. It's better and safer for young pitchers to strive for accuracy and the ability to change velocity than to risk injury by attempting to throw curve balls.

45 PITCHER FIELDING A BUNT

PURPOSE

To familiarize the pitcher with coming off the pitcher's mound after the windup to field a bunted or hit baseball in front of the home-plate area

EQUIPMENT

A ball, a bat, gloves

TIME

5 to 10 minutes per pitcher

PROCEDURE

1. Set up the drill with a pitcher, catcher, infielders, and batter.
2. The pitcher throws the ball, and the batter bunts it toward third base.
3. The pitcher fields the ball in what is sometimes called "no man's land." No man's land is the area between the pitcher, the catcher, and the third baseman. Sometimes, when the ball is bunted into this area, it is too far from the catcher and third baseman for them to field it easily, so the pitcher has the best play.

KEY POINTS

This fielding play for pitchers is important and becomes even more so when the team plays in the playoffs or when a player makes an all-star team.

1. The pitcher should make sure that no matter what the batter does, swing away or square to bunt, the pitching motion doesn't change. Some youth players get rattled when a player squares to bunt and lose focus on the pitch.
2. When fielding a bunted ball the pitcher should run off the mound, keep his eyes on the ball, and pick it up with his glove if it is still moving or with a bare hand if the ball has stopped. The pitcher should plant the front foot and throw the ball to the first baseman.

RELATED DRILLS

22, 69, 70

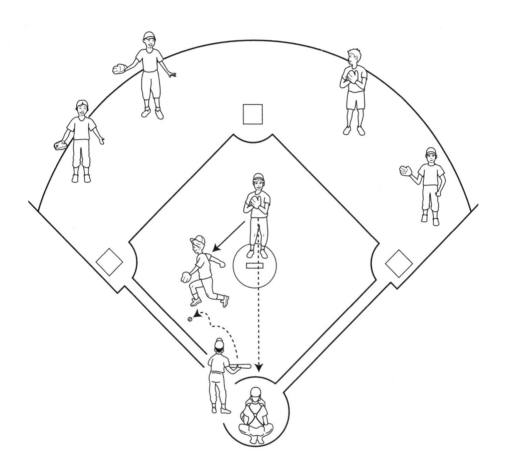

46 PITCHER HOLDING A RUNNER AT THIRD OR SECOND

PURPOSE

To teach the pitcher to hold an unforced runner when fielding the ball

EQUIPMENT

Two baseballs, a bat, gloves

TIME

5 to 10 minutes or until all pitchers are rotated into the drill

PROCEDURE

1. Place a runner on third base and a batter with a bat in the batter's box. Other players take their positions in the field.
2. The pitcher pitches the ball.
3. To speed up the drill the batter does not swing, but instead, as the ball is pitched, the coach throws a grounder to the pitcher, simulating a batted ball. The batter runs to first.
4. The pitcher fields the ball and before throwing the batter out at first, "looks back" the base runner at third to make sure he does not advance off the base too far.
5. The pitcher throws the ball to first base to make the out.

KEY POINTS

This drill should be done during practice the day before a game.

1. The pitcher should wait for the base runner to take a step back toward third base before throwing the ball to first.
2. The pitcher can take a step toward third to "press" the base runner to commit quickly.
3. This drill can also be done with a runner at second base with no force-out.
4. Players should practice what to do when the base runner leads off the base too far. In this situation, the pitcher should run toward the third-base runner and get him into a rundown.

RELATED DRILLS

22, 69, 70

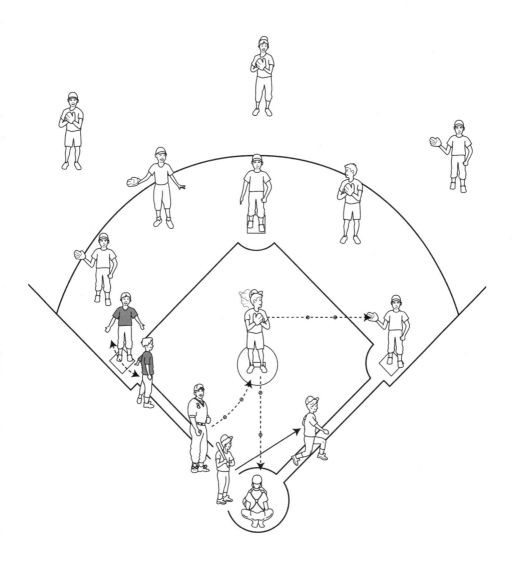

LONG TOSS

PURPOSE

To develop arm strength and accuracy

EQUIPMENT

One ball for each pair of players, gloves

TIME

6 to 8 minutes

PROCEDURE

1. Divide the team into pairs. Partners should be of similar age and skill level.
2. Players stand facing each other approximately 30 feet apart. Increase the distance as the season progresses.
3. Each pair has a baseball. On the "go" command, one partner throws to the other, and when the coach yells, "Go" a second time the partners throw the ball back.
4. Players move back 5 to 10 steps after each pair of throws.
5. Coaches should move up and down the line to make sure players are using correct throwing form, specifically the follow-through.
6. When the players are 80 to 100 feet apart or more, encourage smaller players or those who are not as strong to get the ball to their partner on one bounce.
7. A variation is for everyone to try to reach their partners on one bounce. Then try two bounces.

KEY POINTS

This drill is now recognized as one of the best methods for strengthening a player's throwing arm.

1. Players should "crow hop" before throwing the ball to gain extra power for the throw. The crow hop is a small hop that a fielder makes just before throwing, in order to gain momentum.

2. Coaches should monitor this drill closely and ask if anyone's arm hurts. Players with sore arms should stop the drill. When they've recovered, they can build up strength more gradually.

3. Increase the distance and number of throws as the season progresses.

Variation

Players throw to their partners, as in the standard drill, but if a pair makes a bad throw, that team sits down. The drill continues until just one pair is left.

RELATED DRILLS

49, 50, 51

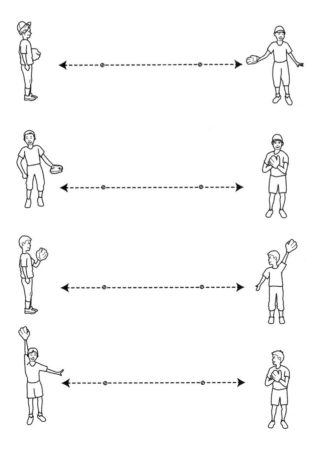

48 TEAM FLAT-SURFACE PITCHING

PURPOSE

To improve the pitching windup

EQUIPMENT

None

TIME

4 to 6 minutes

PROCEDURE

1. All the pitchers line up next to each other on one of the white lines on the field with about 10 or more feet between each player.
2. On the "go" command, the players wind up using the white line as the pitching rubber.
3. Their first step back (six to eight inches) should be with the foot opposite the pitching arm.
4. The players pivot toward the side (the nonthrowing shoulder should face home) and then lift the front leg.
5. The players then drop forward using the lower torso to generate hip rotation.
6. The players repeat this motion several times very slowly.
7. In the middle of the windup, when the opposite leg is lifted, pitchers can freeze and try to maintain a balanced position for several seconds.

KEY POINTS

Going through the pitching motion on a flat surface is a great way for pitchers to concentrate on technique. Practicing without having a ball also forces players to focus on technique only.

1. The player's front leg should be as high or higher than the waist.
2. To achieve complete hip rotation, the front foot faces home plate when it lands.

3. After the player releases the imaginary ball, the throwing hand should end up next to the knee of the opposite leg.

4. If players cannot hold the balanced position, they might have to lower the leg or adjust the initial step back.

5. Players can also perform this drill with closed eyes.

RELATED DRILLS

50, 51

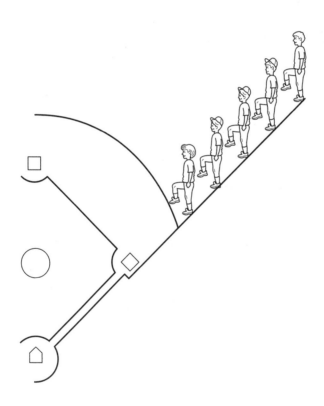

49 BALANCE DRILL

PURPOSE

To improve pitching balance

EQUIPMENT

A bucket of balls

TIME

2 to 4 minutes per pitcher

PROCEDURE

1. One pitcher climbs the mound.
2. The coach stands behind the pitcher with a baseball.
3. The pitcher begins the windup, and as he lifts his front leg, the coach yells, "Hold it."
4. The pitcher holds the position as the coach counts out four or five seconds.
5. The coach hands the ball to the pitcher, who is still in the balanced upright position.
6. The pitcher continues the windup and throws the ball to the target whether it is a net or the catcher.

KEY POINTS

Balance is one of the most important aspects of proper pitching motion. A pitcher cannot throw accurately if he is off balance during the windup. This drill, along with its variations, can be difficult for many youth pitchers. If your players have trouble with this drill, start them on flat ground and build up to the mound.

1. The front leg should be as high or higher than the pitcher's waist in the balanced position.
2. The knee that the player is lifting should not be behind the pitcher's body. In other words, when the pitcher pivots and lifts his front leg, it should be about parallel to the rubber.

3. If the player has trouble holding this position, he should start out lifting the leg only slightly and progress to the proper height over time.

4. Before the coach hands the pitcher the ball, the pitcher reaches back with his throwing arm toward the coach, who places the ball in the pitcher's hand. The player's hand should be on top of the ball.

Variations

1. The player holds the balanced position for a second or two, does a deep-knee bend on one leg while maintaining balance, then rises and throws the ball at the target, which can be a net or a catcher.

2. From the balanced position, the player hops three or four steps toward home plate before throwing the ball.

RELATED DRILLS

48, 51

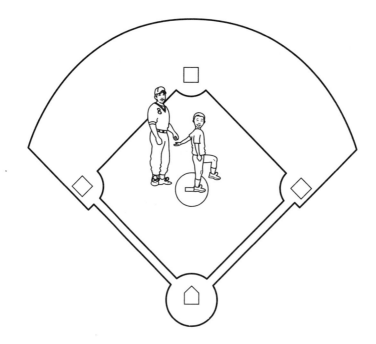

ONE-KNEE DRILL

PURPOSE

To teach players which parts of the body are instrumental in pitching a baseball

EQUIPMENT

One baseball for each pair of players, gloves

TIME

3 to 6 minutes

PROCEDURE

1. Pair up the players.
2. Players form two lines 15 to 20 feet apart. Players in each line should have sufficient space that they don't interfere with each other.
3. Players kneel on one knee (right if they throw right-handed; left if they throw left-handed) with the lead foot pointed directly at their partner.
4. On the "go" command, the partners throw back and forth.
5. After a few minutes, the coach instructs one of the lines to move back a few steps.
6. The players continue throwing.

KEY POINTS

One of the most important things to teach young players is that several parts of the body work together to create the throwing movement. Many beginners falsely believe that only a strong arm is needed to throw a baseball. Players must learn that their legs and hips are also important components for throwing the baseball. By limiting the body parts used in the pitching motion, young players will get a better understanding of what is essential to the whole motion.

1. The player should bring the arm behind the body.
2. Both of the player's arms should be above the shoulder.

3. The player releases the ball in front of the face as the throwing arm extends toward the target.

4. On the follow-through, the pitcher's throwing hand should end up on the outside of the opposite knee.

5. Players should concentrate on throwing strikes to their partner.

Variations

1. The players can do the same drill on both knees to limit the pitching motion to just the upper body; this shows how important the legs are in throwing a baseball.

2. Line up the players side by side and place 5 to 10 cones approximately 30 feet apart from one another in front of the players. See who can knock down the most cones while kneeling.

RELATED DRILLS

48, 49

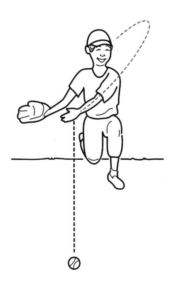

51 THROWING FROM BEHIND THE MOUND

PURPOSE

To develop the correct throwing form, with emphasis on a good follow-through

EQUIPMENT

A bucket of baseballs

TIME

3 to 6 minutes

PROCEDURE

1. Place a pitcher with a bucket of balls on the pitcher's mound behind the rubber on the second-base side of the diamond.
2. Standing at the edge of the dirt, the pitcher throws either to a catcher or to a screen at home plate.

KEY POINTS

Throwing uphill forces the pitcher to isolate the follow-through portion of the pitch and concentrate on it more than when pitching off the downhill slope or on flat ground.

1. The pitcher should take the normal step back when beginning the windup.
2. Shorten the distance to the catcher or screen to 40 to 45 feet if the pitcher has trouble throwing from this location to home plate.
3. When pitching uphill, the pitcher may tend to drag the back leg. Therefore, remind the pitcher to lift the back leg as in a normal windup.
4. Because throwing strikes is not a priority in this drill, pitchers should throw into a large screen rather than aiming for a target.
5. Because it is difficult to throw uphill while the legs are straight, this drill forces pitchers to bend the knees during the windup.

6. When following through, the pitcher's throwing hand should finish at the side of the opposite knee.

Variation

This drill is just as effective on any hill.

RELATED DRILLS

48, 49, 50

5

Baserunning Drills

Most youth baseball coaches are aware of the importance of throwing, hitting, fielding, and pitching; these skills are obviously important. However, many coaches underestimate the value of smart and aggressive baserunning. But, youth teams that practice baserunning skills often earn one or two extra runs per game with their aggressive style. Earning extra bases or runs can make a hero out of a player who might not hit for power. Youth coaches sometimes learn that the fastest players are not necessarily the best base runners, and even in the youngest groups, players can surprise their coach with their instincts.

Another benefit of learning baserunning techniques and practicing them is that it teaches young players to pay attention to what is happening on the base path instead of simply going through the motions. Concentrating on the base paths increases a player's concentration span. For these reasons, youth coaches should devote 5 to 10 minutes of every practice to baserunning.

The drills in this chapter highlight the most important techniques. For instance, base runners should bounce off of the base on every pitch. This bouncing technique prepares the base runner to take off in the event of a wild pitch or if the coach gives the sign to steal. Other drills reinforce baserunning cliches such as, "When you hit the ball, do not look at it. Just run."

Coaches who practice and reinforce baserunning techniques will be pleased with how a player's skills transfer to game situations. And coaches should not back away from aggressive baserunning during games, even if their players are sometimes thrown out; assertiveness often spreads to other parts of their game.

Because fielders and base runners converge at the bases, often at a sprint, coaches must teach players how to play safely. Base runners must wear helmets on base, and players should be taught to slide into any base (except first) if there will be a play there. These safety lessons can be honed during practice, then carried over into games.

We have all seen young players make avoidable and embarrassing mistakes on the bases. Well-coached teams rarely make such mistakes because they focus on baserunning skills during practice. Their players have developed the foresight to predict the actions of defensive players and can use that foresight to avoid most baserunning blunders.

Many major league teams spend little time on baserunning. Apart from the first or third base coach telling them what to do, professional athletes are guided by their instincts. Baserunning drills will help youth players develop the instincts that will serve them well at their current level and beyond.

THREE-BASE SLIDING

PURPOSE

To develop proper sliding techniques

EQUIPMENT

Three loose bases

TIME

3 to 6 minutes

PROCEDURE

1. Place three bases spaced at least 10 feet apart in a grassy area out in foul territory.
2. Divide players into three lines, one line 45 to 60 feet behind each base.
3. Players should not wear cleats for this drill. (This is a safety precaution.)
4. On the "go" command, the first player in each line runs and slides into the base.
5. After sliding, the player returns to the end of the line, and the next person in line slides.

KEY POINTS

1. When players slide, they must not start the slide too early or too late; depending on their age and size, players should begin the slide when they are about three to five feet from the base.
2. Players should lift their hands over their heads when sliding to prevent hand injuries.
3. On the slide, the trail leg bends dramatically 45 degrees or even more while the lead leg bends slightly.

Variations

1. Use large sliding mats for indoor practices.

2. Put down a plastic or vinyl tarp on the outfield grass, water it thoroughly, and let the kids take off their shoes and slide on it. These steps reduce the chances of injury. Players slide a long way so that coaches can get a good look at technique, and the players have a great time.

RELATED DRILL

55

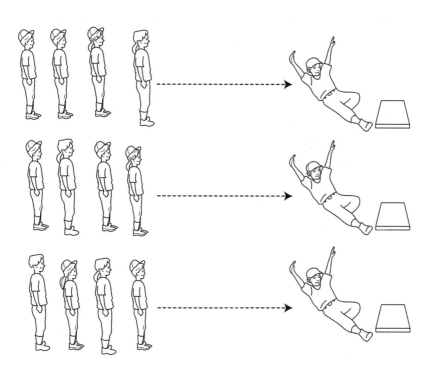

53   TAGGING UP

PURPOSE

To develop proper tagging-up techniques

EQUIPMENT

Three bases, a baseball, gloves

TIME

4 to 6 minutes

PROCEDURE

1. Set up three bases in the shape of a baseball diamond.
2. Place three fielders in the outfield positions. A coach stands in the infield between the pitcher's mound and second base.
3. The rest of the team lines up at first base.
4. The first player in line leads off first base a few feet. The coach throws a fly ball to one of the outfielders, and when the outfielder catches the ball, the player runs back to first base, tags up, then hustles to second base.
5. Although the outfielder attempts to catch every ball, he does not throw out any of the base runners as they tag up and run to the next base.
6. The first player stays at second base. The next player in line at first base repeats the drill, but this time, both runners on base tag up. Now the bases are loaded for the third throw, and all three runners tag up on it. Repeat the drill for every player.
7. The coach rotates the throws to the different outfielders.
8. After everyone has had a chance to run at least twice, the fielders come in and three new players head to the outfield.

KEY POINTS

Tagging up and advancing at the youth level takes a combination of good judgment and proper baserunning and sliding techniques. Coaches should explain the different leads and that choosing which one to use depends on which base the player is on and where the ball is hit.

1. Players should not lead off the base too far.

2. Players must wait for the ball to be caught before running. Runners say, "Caught" out loud when the ball is caught as a reminder not to run too early.

3. When tagging up, the runner should not run with the head up looking for the incoming throw. He should run with his head looking directly at the base he is advancing to.

4. Teach players to slide into the bag they are advancing to after a tag up almost every time.

5. When tagging up from third base, the player never leads. He should stay on the base until the ball is caught.

RELATED DRILLS

55, 56, 57, 58, 59

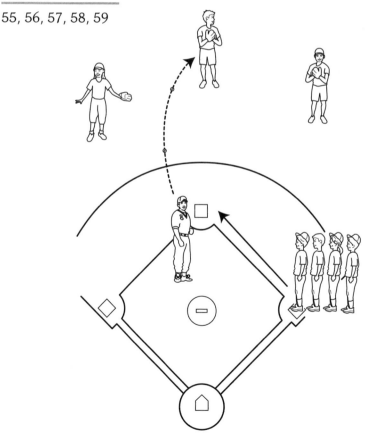

BOUNCE AND RUN

PURPOSE

To develop aggressive baserunning tactics

EQUIPMENT

A couple of baseballs, gloves

TIME

5 to 10 minutes

PROCEDURE

1. Place a first baseman, shortstop, and third baseman around the infield.
2. A player stands on second base, and the rest of the players line up on the outfield side of the base behind him.
3. A coach stands between home plate and first base, closer to home plate than to first.
4. The coach throws a ground ball to either shortstop or third base.
5. The player on second base bounces off the base, and when the fielder throws the ball to first base, runs to third.
6. The next in line enters the drill. The runner now at third base does the same thing he did at second base, but this time runs home after the fielder throws to first.
7. After running home, the player goes to the end of the line at second base.

KEY POINTS

In youth baseball, teams can scratch out as many as two extra runs a game with aggressive baserunning. However, this aggressiveness must first be practiced; therefore, you should schedule this drill for every practice. In this drill, there is no force-out at any base; there is either a runner at second base or third base or both with fewer than two outs.

1. The runner should bounce off the base with knees bent.

2. If the grounder is thrown to the shortstop, the runner's lead at second base should not be as large as it would be if the grounder were thrown to third. The runner at third base, however, should bounce farther off the base if the grounder goes to shortstop and stay closer to the base if the ball is thrown to third.

3. When the fielder releases the ball, and not before, runners should sprint with their heads down. Fielders can fake a throw to keep the base runners honest.

4. When the base runner turns to run to the next base, he should not lift his head to look back at the throw.

5. Coaches should randomly alternate throwing grounders to the shortstop and the third baseman.

6. Periodically coaches should bring the fielders in and send three new players to the outfield. Practicing baserunning also teaches defensive players to pay attention to what's going on when they are on base rather than mentally drifting away and committing run-producing errors.

RELATED DRILLS

56, 57, 58, 59

PURPOSE

To practice giving and receiving coaching signs

EQUIPMENT

A baseball, two sets of bases, gloves

TIME

4 to 6 minutes

PROCEDURE

1. Place two bags at each base approximately three feet from each other around the diamond. This allows twice as many players to participate in the drill.
2. A coach stands in the third-base coaching box.
3. The first two players stand on the two parallel first bases.
4. The coach relays a signal to the players.
5. The pitcher throws the ball to the catcher, and the base runners execute the baserunning skill the third-base coach indicates.
6. The first two runners end up at second base. Two new runners begin at first base.

KEY POINTS

This drill serves two purposes: It teaches the baserunning signs, and it lets players get used to timing their jumps on the base path.

1. The signs recommended in this drill are as follows:

   (A) Bounce and hold on the pitcher's throw, (B) steal the next base as soon as the ball crosses home plate, and (C) bounce and delay the steal to the next base until the throw back from the catcher to the pitcher.

2. The pair of base runners stealing home should stop approximately six feet short of the catcher to avoid collisions. Another coach can stand halfway down the base path and act as a marker so that the runners know where to stop.

3. Players should turn their heads and sprint to the next base without looking up.

4. On the delayed steal, base runners should take their bounces without giving away the play. The runners must also make sure that the ball is released from the catcher's hand before stealing the next base. The delayed steal is one of the best and most aggressive baserunning techniques in youth baseball. However, coaches must first determine the ability and speed of the players before attempting it. Coaches must also realize that the fastest base runners are not necessarily the best and that some players have natural instincts and will steal more bases than players who are faster than they are.

RELATED DRILLS

57, 58, 59

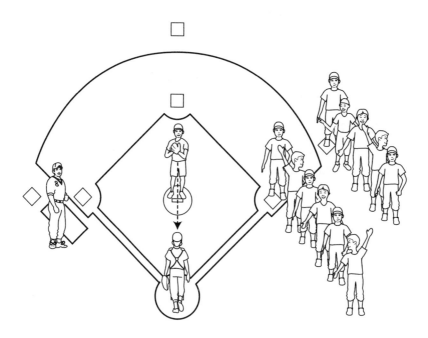

56   HOME TO SECOND

PURPOSE

To develop baserunning techniques for going from home plate to second base on an extra base hit

EQUIPMENT

A baseball, gloves

TIME

3 to 6 minutes or one or two turns for each player

PROCEDURE

1. The players line up at home plate.
2. The coach throws a ball into the outfield between two fielders, simulating an extra base hit.
3. As a fielder is about to field the ball, the coach yells, "Go."
4. The first player in line at home plate runs to first base, rounds the bag, and turns to second base while the fielder gets the ball and throws it to second base.
5. The next player in line enters the drill.
6. After reaching second base, the player returns home without getting in the way of the drill and returns to the end of the line.

KEY POINTS

It is important for players to experience as many baserunning scenarios as possible. This increases overall knowledge and appreciation of the game.

1. Players running to first base should pay attention to the first-base coach.
2. When approaching first base on a hit to the outfield, runners should take a gradual loop into foul territory 6 to 10 feet before approaching the base. This allows runners to successfully round the base without taking too wide a turn. A gradual loop also allows the runner to retain balance and running speed and get a good angle for touching the base. This also gets the player from home to second more quickly.

3. Runners should touch the inner corner of first base when rounding the bag. This should not be difficult if the player takes the loop into foul territory.

4. A player can be tagged out if he overruns second base.

5. Players should get used to sliding most of the time. Younger players sometimes aren't sure if they should go in standing up or sliding in. A coach can assist the runner by yelling out which to do; however, the crowd can drown out the coach's voice. Therefore, the youth player should be taught that when in doubt, slide into the bag.

RELATED DRILLS

55, 58, 59

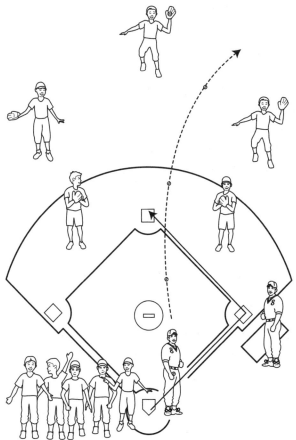

57   FIRST TO THIRD

PURPOSE

To develop baserunning techniques for going from first base to third base on a base hit

EQUIPMENT

A bucket of balls, gloves

TIME

3 to 6 minutes or one or two turns for each player

PROCEDURE

1. Place a right fielder, center fielder, second baseman, short-stop, and third baseman at their respective positions. The rest of the players line up behind first base.
2. The coach, located at the pitcher's mound, throws a ball into the outfield between the center fielder and the right fielder.
3. As the coach throws the ball, he yells, "Go," and the first player in line runs toward second base, touches the inside of the bag, and continues to third.
4. The fielders make a play for the ball and try to throw the runner out at third base.
5. The next player in line enters the drill.
6. The first player jogs back to the end of the line.

KEY POINTS

1. To avoid getting caught in a double play, the player on first base should watch the ball go through the infield before running to second.
2. Players should remember that runners at first will be called out if they're hit with a ball hit to the right side of the field.
3. When running to second base, the player should run hard but slow up enough to touch the inside of the bag. When continuing on to third, runners should remember that a wide turn at second will slow them down.

4. When running to third base, the runner should look at and listen to the coach, who will indicate whether to go into the base standing up or sliding in.

5. Runners can be tagged out if they overrun third base.

Variation

Once in a while, the coach should throw the ball to one of the infielders on a fly. If the players are studying the movement of the ball before they run, then they should know not to run on a fly ball or line drive right to a fielder.

RELATED DRILLS

55, 56, 59

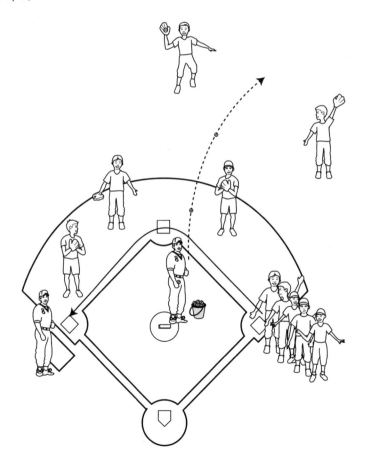

58   SECOND TO HOME

PURPOSE

To develop baserunning techniques for going from second base to home plate on a base hit

EQUIPMENT

A bucket of balls, gloves

TIME

3 to 6 minutes or one or two turns for each player

PROCEDURE

1. Place a right fielder, center fielder, second baseman, shortstop, and catcher at their respective positions. The rest of the players line up at second base.
2. The coach, located at the pitcher's mound, throws a ball into the outfield between two outfielders.
3. As the coach throws the ball, he yells, "Go," and the first player in line runs toward third, touches the bag, and heads home.
4. The fielders try to throw the runner out at home. The runner then jogs back to the end of the line at second base.
5. The next player in line enters the drill.

KEY POINTS

1. Players running from second base to third base have a big advantage because they are also running toward the third-base coach, who gives instructions on whether to stay at third, go home, or round the base and hold.
2. The "round the base and hold" technique is used if the coach cannot determine whether to send the runner or not. However, if the ball is misplayed on the relay into the infield, the runner, who holds about 6 to 10 feet off third, is in a good position to run home on the coach's command.

3. If the coach tells the runner to go home, the player should not take too wide a turn around third base; however, runners should know that they are allowed to run into foul territory as they round third.

4. Base runners should almost always slide at home to avoid a collision with the catcher.

RELATED DRILLS

55, 56, 57

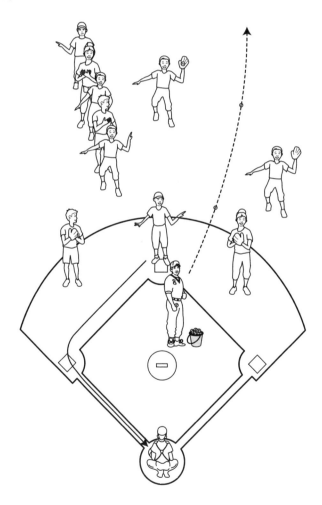

6

Game Situation Drills

As in the game of chess, there are a seemingly endless number of plays that occur in youth baseball games. However, several of these game situations reappear frequently. Practicing specific plays teaches players what they should do in a particular situation. This knowledge eliminates the guesswork during a game. Coaches can, and should, drill the team on both the common and the rare game situations. Players are far more likely to react quickly and correctly to both types of situations if they have encountered them in practice.

Determining who becomes a backup and who takes the cutoff in specific scenarios should be practiced often. When simulating game situations, be sure to station base runners, then rotate the base runners with the fielders to give everyone a chance at both offense and defense. In youth baseball, one of the most common situations teams find themselves in is the "first and third" steal situation. Some coaches try to teach their teams 10 or 12 different plays for this situation, but this confuses players and can be counterproductive, especially when working with kids 10 to 12 years old. Coaches should try to make this play as simple for the players as possible, especially when playing defense.

Another crucial game situation for fielders and base runners is knowing what to do with the ball after it is hit. The answer depends upon several factors that young players must learn to keep track of: the number of outs, the inning, the score, who the ball is hit to, and who the base runner is. Youth players are often confused by all of the factors influencing the situation, especially when coaches, parents, and infielders yell different things. One solution for players still learning the game is for outfielders to throw the ball to the closest infielder wearing the same color uniform. Simplified? Yes, but it is effective.

The practice the day after a game is the best time to go over game situations. You don't have to review the entire game, but instead, walk the team through two or three situations that stand out. This will help players understand what happened and will prepare them for the next game. When practicing game situation drills, don't schedule more than two per practice.

The skill level of a team will determine how advanced the game situations used in practice should be. Not all teams will be ready to take advantage of all the options available to them, especially when it comes to fielding. There is absolutely nothing wrong with a team using its most skilled player or players to make diving catches or take cutoffs. The youth coach must be flexible.

59   CALLING TIME-OUT

PURPOSE

To learn the proper way to call time-out during a game

EQUIPMENT

A bat

TIME

4 to 6 minutes

PROCEDURE

1. Each player stands in the batter's box with a catcher. The coach is the umpire.
2. Before the pitcher throws the ball, the player must call time-out.
3. After everyone completes this half of the drill, the players move to second base. One at a time, they run and slide at third base.
4. The player calls time-out after sliding.

KEY POINTS

This drill is more important than you might think. Many young players are used to their backyard games and think that once they call time-out it is automatically given to them.

1. Players must learn that when they are on the base they must ask for time from the umpire. They should not move until the umpire grants it.
2. This drill works best with a real umpire in uniform if you can find one willing to participate.
3. The umpire should occasionally not grant the players a time-out. See how they react.

RELATED DRILLS

61, 62, 63, 64, 65, 66, 67, 68, 69

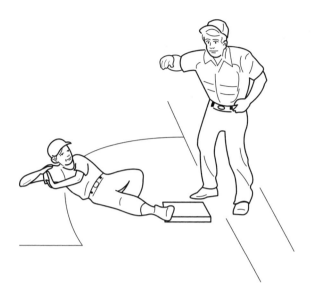

DEFEND STEAL OF SECOND

PURPOSE

To develop defensive strategies against a base runner advancing to second base on a steal.

EQUIPMENT

One baseball, a bat, gloves

TIME

6 to 8 minutes

PROCEDURE

1. A player stands on first base, and a batter is in the batter's box.
2. The pitcher pitches the baseball.
3. When the ball crosses the plate the base runner runs to second base.
4. The catcher throws the ball to second base.
5. The shortstop covers the base and tries to tag the runner out.

KEY POINTS

Throwing out a runner trying to steal second base is an important play, but teams rarely practice it.

1. After the pitcher throws the ball, the runner at first starts for second base, and the shortstop covers the bag for the throw from the catcher. Some coaches take into account whether the batter is right-handed or left-handed when deciding who should cover second base. However, it's best to keep it simple and practice this play one way.
2. The second baseman backs up the shortstop three to five feet behind the base.
3. The catcher throws the ball to second base, throwing to the base and not to the shortstop covering it.

4. The center fielder serves as a second backup to the second baseman; however, he should not come in so close that the ball passes him on an overthrow.

5. If the ball does go past the shortstop and the second baseman, the center fielder should control the ball, run it back into the infield, and hand it to one of the infielders.

RELATED DRILLS

62, 63, 64, 65, 66, 67, 68, 69, 70

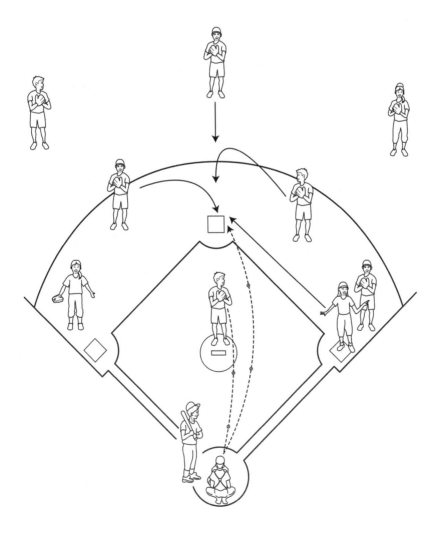

61   BUNT WITH MAN ON THIRD

PURPOSE

To stress the importance of bunting as a crucial run-producing tactic

EQUIPMENT

One baseball, a bat, gloves

TIME

6 to 8 minutes

PROCEDURE

1. One player is in the batter's box; the other players take their infield positions, and a base runner leads off of third.
2. The pitcher throws the ball, and the batter bunts the ball toward third base.
3. The base runner bounces off third base.
4. The third baseman fields the ball and throws it to first.
5. The base runner breaks for home as the third baseman lets go of the ball.

KEY POINTS

1. The base runner should bounce off the base quickly.
2. Where the ball is bunted determines how far the base runner should bounce off the base.
3. The base runner must react quickly and break for home as soon as the ball leaves the fielder's hand.
4. The base runner should run directly home, not look back at the ball, and slide.

RELATED DRILLS

60, 63, 64, 65, 66, 67, 68, 69, 70

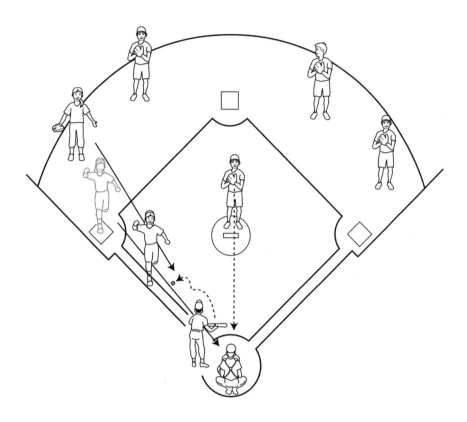

62 DEFEND BUNT WITH MAN ON THIRD

PURPOSE

To develop defensive strategies against a runner on third trying to score on a bunt

EQUIPMENT

One baseball, a bat, gloves

TIME

6 to 8 minutes

PROCEDURE

1. The pitcher throws the baseball, and the batter bunts toward third.
2. The third baseman fields the ball.
3. The base runner anticipates the throw to first and begins to run home.
4. The third baseman fields the ball, wheels around and immediately throws it to the shortstop covering third base. The shortstop applies the tag to the base runner who is trying to scramble back to third.

KEY POINTS

1. Timing in this drill is important.
2. As the base runner bounces off the base, the shortstop sneaks over to cover third.
3. To remind the shortstop to cover third, the coach yells out a signal, such as, "Green," as the third baseman charges to field the bunt.
4. Upon hearing the coach yell, "Green," the third baseman quickly turns and throws to the shortstop covering third base.
5. The left fielder backs up the shortstop in case the ball is overthrown. If the play is backed up correctly, a run can be saved.

RELATED DRILLS

60, 61, 64, 65, 66, 67, 68, 69, 70

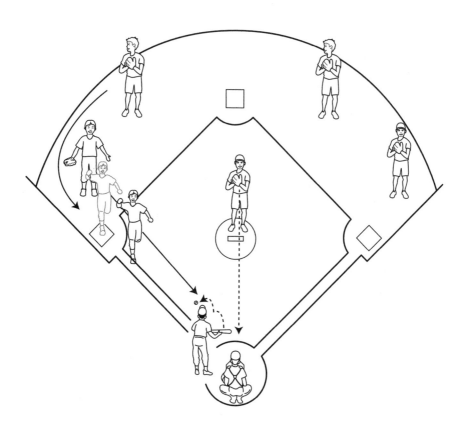

63 FIRST-AND-THIRD OFFENSIVE SITUATION

PURPOSE

To develop defensive strategies against a first-and-third steal situation

EQUIPMENT

One baseball, a bat, gloves

TIME

6 to 10 minutes

PROCEDURE

1. Set up infielders.
2. Station base runners on first and third.
3. The pitcher throws the ball, and when the ball crosses the plate, the runner on first runs to second.
4. Depending on how the defense is set up, what the score is, and what inning it is, the runner at third will either stay or run home.

KEY POINTS

1. The batter should take the pitch so that the runners can move up.
2. The runner at first base must slide at second whether the catcher throws the ball or not. Sliding creates a bigger diversion for the fielders than going in standing up.
3. The runner at third base should bounce off the base toward home plate and constantly look at the catcher.
4. If the catcher fakes a throw down, the base runner on third should stay on the base. Although the third-base runner doesn't advance, at least one base runner moves up and no one is thrown out.
5. If the catcher throws the ball to second base, the base runner on third must watch the flight of the ball. Sometimes the catcher throws hard back to the pitcher to make it look like

he is throwing it all the way to second base. In this case, the pitcher can throw to third and catch the base runner too far off the base.

6. Other times, the catcher may make it look like he's throwing to second base, but he will throw it to a drawn-in short-stop or second baseman. If the shortstop or second baseman catches the ball, the base runner must go back to third base.

7. If the ball goes all the way to second base, then the base runner at third can take off and slide into home plate.

8. If the coach determines that the fielding team has excellent skills, the base runner on first can stop between first and second. A rundown will ensue, which might allow enough time for the runner on third base to score.

RELATED DRILLS

60, 61, 62, 65, 66, 69, 70

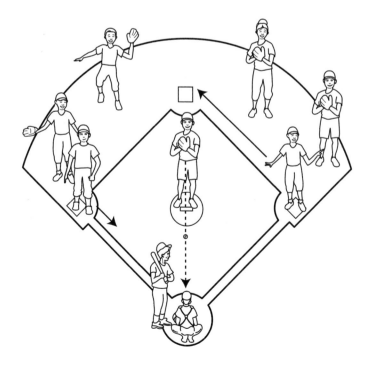

64 FIRST-AND-THIRD DEFENSIVE SITUATION

PURPOSE

To learn to contain runners at first and third without sacrificing a run

EQUIPMENT

One baseball, gloves

TIME

6 to 10 minutes

PROCEDURE

1. Set up the infield, and station runners on first and third bases
2. The pitcher pitches the ball, and when it crosses the plate, the runner on first base runs to second.
3. The defensive team tries to contain the base runners without giving up a run.

KEY POINTS

Although the first-and-third steal play is difficult to defend, there are many options to prevent the play from succeeding.

1. One option is for the coach to set up a way to signal to the infielders who should make the play. For instance, the coach can call out the names of three infielders. He can yell out, "First-and-third situation; get ready, Mike, Bob, Don." The second name called has been predetermined to be the player the catcher throws to. When a player's name is called, such as the shortstop's, he takes two steps forward. The catcher throws the ball to him in that position.
2. The shortstop catches the ball and very quickly looks over at third base. He can throw it there if he thinks that the runner is too far off the base.
3. This drill works well for holding the runner; however, it allows the runner on first to steal second.

4. Teams should also practice throwing the runner out at second base. Some offensive teams freeze if they aren't expecting a throw down to the base.

5. If the player at third base has too much of a lead, the defensive team should quickly throw to that base to try to pick off the runner. If the shortstop receives the throw from the catcher, he can run toward third base, forcing the runner to go back to third or run home. Running at the base runner is also a fundamentally sound defensive tactic for youth fielders.

6. If the second baseman receives the throw from the catcher, or if the base runner has too big a lead for the shortstop to chase down, the fielder must throw the ball to third base. The fielders should not rush their throws. If they are in motion when fielding the ball, they must stop, plant their feet, and then throw an accurate strike to the third baseman or catcher, depending on how far down the line the base runner is.

RELATED DRILLS

60, 61, 62, 63, 66, 67, 68, 69, 70

65

DELAYED STEAL

PURPOSE

To develop offensive strategies to advance a base runner

EQUIPMENT

One baseball, gloves

TIME

6 to 10 minutes with players rotating in and out of the drill.

PROCEDURE

1. Place defensive players in the infield. Line up the rest of players behind first base with the first player on the base.
2. The pitcher throws the ball.
3. As the catcher throws the ball back to the pitcher, the base runner bounces off the bag, runs, and slides into second base.
4. The next player in line enters the drill, and the runner who went to second base performs the drill at third.
5. The player on third base tries a delayed steal to home.

KEY POINTS

A player performs a delayed steal after the pitch and on the catcher's anticipated throw back to the pitcher. The base runner leads off the base in a subtle but calculated fashion by sneaking off the base inches at a time, while also appearing disinterested in taking the next base. When the catcher throws the ball back to the pitcher, the base runner takes off for the next base as soon as the ball leaves the catcher's hand. The coach should teach players to look for the following situations when deciding to attempt a delayed steal.

1. If the pitcher retrieves the ball from the catcher at the top of the mound instead of the base of the mound, this gives the base runner more time to steal before the pitcher receives the ball.

2. If the catcher falls to his knees when throwing the ball to the pitcher, the throw will not be as hard, which gives the base runner more time to steal.

3. If the catcher lobs a "rainbow" back to the pitcher instead of a hard, direct throw, the throw will take longer to reach the pitcher.

RELATED DRILLS

60, 61, 62, 63, 64, 67, 68, 69, 70

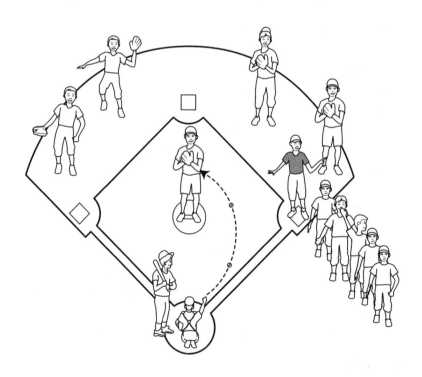

66

DEFEND DELAYED STEAL

PURPOSE

To develop defensive strategies to prevent players from advancing on a delayed steal

EQUIPMENT

One baseball, a bat, gloves

TIME

6 to 10 minutes

PROCEDURE

1. Place a runner on first base, and assign the players to different fielding positions.
2. After the pitch, the base runner bounces off the bag ready to attempt the delayed steal if the opportunity presents itself.
3. The defenders react according to the actions of the base runner.
4. After every pitch, the pitcher comes to the base of the mound to retrieve the ball. Once he has possession of the ball, he looks the base runner back to first.
5. The catcher stands up after every pitch before throwing the ball back to the pitcher.
6. The catcher throws a line drive back to the pitcher, not a rainbow-type throw.
7. If the catcher thinks the base runner has too big a lead at first, he runs at the base runner and forces him back to the bag.
8. Rotate the players around the different fielding positions.

KEY POINT

To prevent the delayed steal from first, players must learn and practice certain procedures and techniques whenever players are on base. The catcher can throw behind the runner in a pick-off attempt, but the outfielder must be in a position to back him up.

RELATED DRILLS

60, 61, 62, 63, 64, 65, 68, 69, 70

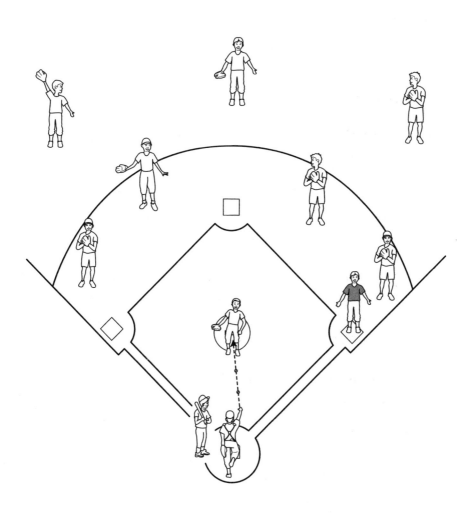

67 PREVENT ADVANCEMENT ON GROUND BALL

PURPOSE

To develop strategies for keeping a runner on first base from advancing to third on a ground ball after getting the batter out at first

EQUIPMENT

One baseball, a bat, gloves

TIME

4 to 6 minutes

PROCEDURE

1. Place a runner on first base and a batter in the batter's box.
2. The coach throws a ground ball to an infielder.
3. The infielder, instead of trying to make the out at second base (the runner is too fast), throws to first base for the sure out.
4. The first baseman catches the ball and runs toward third base to prevent the runner at second from advancing.
5. If the runner tries to advance to third, the first baseman stops, plants his foot, and throws to third.
6. If the runner does not try to advance, the first baseman keeps his eye on the base runner and hands the baseball to the pitcher while the pitcher's foot is still on the mound.

KEY POINTS

Although this drill is primarily for the first baseman, it is important for the entire team to understand this play.

1. The first baseman must not take his foot off the bag too quickly.
2. The first baseman should go in front of the pitcher's mound when running to third.

RELATED DRILLS

60, 61, 62, 63, 64, 65, 66, 69, 70

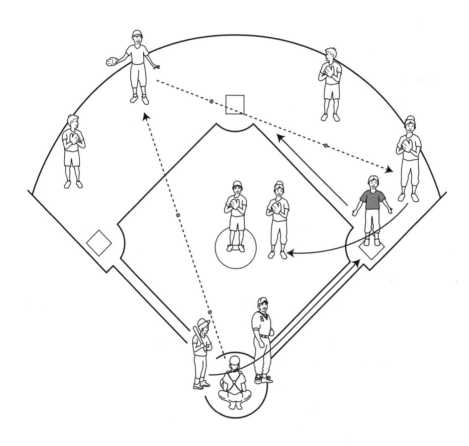

68 BASES LOADED FORCE-OUT AT HOME

PURPOSE

To develop defensive tactics for making the force-out at home plate with two outs and the bases loaded

EQUIPMENT

One baseball, a bat, gloves

TIME

4 to 6 minutes, rotating pitchers

PROCEDURE

1. Set up a complete infield, including the pitcher and catcher, and place runners at each base, including home plate.
2. The coach stands in the batter's box and hits a slow ground ball to the pitcher.
3. The player on home runs out of the batter's box toward first base.
4. Where and how the pitcher fields the ball determines whether he should make the force-out at home or not.

KEY POINTS

There is a force-out at every base when the bases are loaded. In a bases-loaded situation with two outs, players are usually taught to make the throw to first base; however, in some situations, that may not be the easiest throw to make.

1. Pitchers should throw the ball to the catcher underhanded for the force-out at home if they have fielded the ball cleanly and their momentum takes them toward home plate.
2. The pitcher should aim for the catcher's chest.
3. If a pitcher's momentum takes him all the way to home plate after fielding the ball, he should continue to run home and step on the plate for the out. A pitcher should only run all the way to home plate if he knows he can make the out.

RELATED DRILLS

60, 61, 62, 63, 64, 65, 66, 67, 70

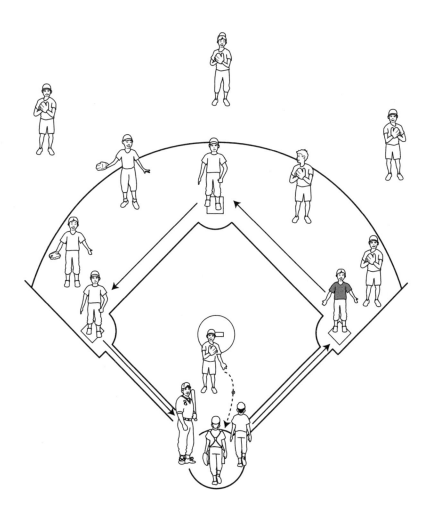

PURPOSE

To develop defensive tactics for a pitcher covering first base on a ball hit to the right side of the infield

EQUIPMENT

A ball, gloves

TIME

4 to 8 minutes or rotation of players

PROCEDURE

1. Set up the right side of the infield with a first baseman, a second baseman, and a pitcher. The pitcher stands at the base of the mound.
2. Perform the drill first without a base runner.
3. The coach, standing at home plate, throws a slow ground ball somewhere between first and second base.
4. The first baseman charges the ball as the pitcher runs over to cover first base.
5. The first baseman tosses the ball to the pitcher, leading the pitcher with the ball to first base.
6. The second baseman runs toward first base to back up the throw.

KEY POINTS

This scenario, which frequently occurs in youth baseball, is difficult to master. Players should also know when a play like this occurs during games so that they are ready.

1. When fielding the ball, the first baseman should lead the pitcher to first base with an underhand throw toward the vacated base and not at the pitcher running to the bag.
2. If the ball is bunted down the first-base line and the pitcher gets to the ball before the first baseman does (he is charging to field the ball), the second baseman must cover first base.

3. Practice this drill first without a base runner.

4. Sometimes the catcher can field a slow bunt or a ground ball.

5. Coaches should rotate players, especially pitchers.

RELATED DRILLS

60, 61, 62, 63, 64, 65, 66, 67, 68, 71

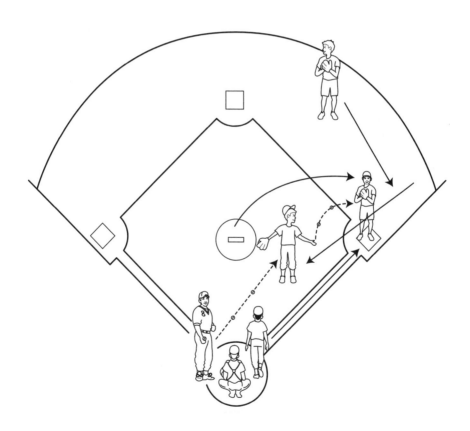

7

Warm-Up and Cool-Down Drills

With so much emphasis on improving skills and learning plays, it's easy for coaches and players to forget that baseball practice should be fun. That's where games come into play. Almost any backyard game can be modified for an organized baseball practice. Creative baseball-related drills are not only informative but also are loads of fun for players, coaches, and parents. These "warm-up and cool-down" drills are perfect for the beginning of the season, and players should be familiar with them at every early practice. Younger teams should play at least one of these games at each practice throughout the season. Older players can play these games before the start of the season to review basic baseball skills. These games also provide a change of pace to a stale practice.

Coaches typically schedule these games for the beginning or end of practice, but you can and should use them in the middle of practice following a tedious teaching situation. Remember, the main objective for these games is to begin or end practice on a high note or to break up a practice with a different activity. Usually by the middle of the season, a team has settled on a particular game it likes best, and players ask to play it. Use this game as a reward for a good practice or as an incentive to keep working hard. Players will practice with greater efficiency and greater concentration if they know that they can earn a chance to play their favorite game.

Young players love competition. To keep competition in perspective, it is important that all players experience winning and losing during the season. To make sure that happens, coaches should divide the players into teams instead of letting the players do it themselves. As we've all seen, when players choose teams, the same two or three are often selected last, which can affect these players negatively. Similarly, coaches should select drills that highlight different skills so that many players have a chance to shine.

Coaches should also devise games that are not directly related to baseball. There is no better way to relax an 11- and 12-year-old playoff or all-star team than to introduce silly, nonstressful, and warm-up and cool-down games during practice. Coaches should evaluate which of these games work best for their teams.

These drills can also function as a change of pace following hard work on another drill. Using a fun drill after a harder drill can be very effective in stimulating and re-energizing young players. Though we refer to these drills as warm-up and cool-down drills, coaches should keep one or two of them available to use when appropriate during practice.

70 BASEBALL TAG

PURPOSE

To develop proper glove technique for squeezing the ball when running to tag an opposing base runner

EQUIPMENT

One or two baseballs in each player's glove, cones or other props to designate the playing field

TIME

3 to 6 minutes

PROCEDURE

1. Mark off the playing area on the baseball diamond.
2. Choose one player to be "it."
3. On the "go" command, the player who is it tries to tag the other players within the confined area without dropping the ball or balls from the glove.
4. A tagged player must sit down. As more and more players are tagged out, the coach moves the cones in to reduce the size of the playing field and to keep the pace of the game quick.

KEY POINT

Players should keep their heads up looking at the player they're chasing and their gloves squeezed tightly as they run with the baseball.

Variations

1. More than one player can be "it." This variation creates more obstacles for the runners to avoid and allows more players to practice running with the baseball.
2. Players can also run with the ball in their bare hands when trying to make a tag.

RELATED DRILLS

None

71   RELAY HANDOFF

PURPOSE

To teach the importance of squeezing the baseball in the glove while running

EQUIPMENT

One ball for each line of players, gloves

TIME

3 to 6 minutes

PROCEDURE

1. Divide the team into two (or more) even lines.
2. The first player in each line holds one or two baseballs in the glove.
3. On the "go" command the first player in each line runs to a designated area, turns around, and runs back to his line.
4. After running the course the player hands the baseball to the next person in line. Each person gets a chance to run with the baseball.
5. The first team to finish with the baseball securely maintained in the last runner's glove wins the race.

KEY POINTS

1. Squeezing the ball in their gloves ensures that players don't drop the ball in an intense game situation such as a rundown.
2. Coaches may try two baseballs per line, instead of just one, to speed up the drill.
3. Runners must hand, not throw, the ball to the next person in line.

Variation

Players can also run with the ball in their bare hands.

RELATED DRILLS

None

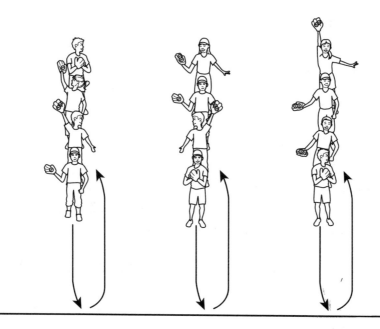

72   STEAL THE BACON

PURPOSE

To develop ball-handling skills

EQUIPMENT

One baseball, gloves

TIME

3 to 10 minutes

PROCEDURE

1. Divide the team into two groups, line them up across from each other, and number the players in each group from one to six.
2. The coach puts a ball between the lines and yells out a number.
3. Both players with this number run toward the ball and try to grab it, or steal the bacon.
4. When one of the players picks up the ball, the other tries to tag him with the glove.
5. The player who picks up the ball tries to run back to the line without getting tagged.
6. Award one team a point if its player gets back to the line without being tagged.
7. Award the other team a point if its player makes the tag before the runner reaches the line.

KEY POINTS

1. As in the relay handoff game, players should squeeze their gloves when carrying the ball.
2. No points are awarded if a player drops the ball during the drill.

Variation

Players can also run with the ball in their bare hands when trying to make a tag.

RELATED DRILLS

None

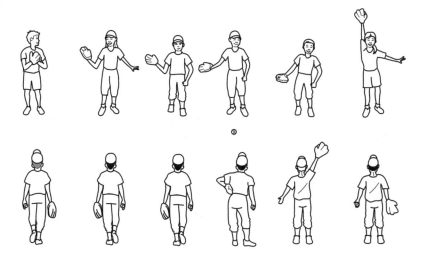

73 BASEBALL RED LIGHT, GREEN LIGHT

PURPOSE

To improve a player's ability to run while wearing a glove

EQUIPMENT

One or two baseballs and a glove per player

TIME

4 to 8 minutes

PROCEDURE

1. One player is the caller, and the other players line up a particular distance away from the caller. The distance varies depending on the age of the players.
2. Every player, except the caller, wears a baseball glove and holds a baseball in it.
3. The caller, facing away from the other players, shouts, "Green light."
4. The other players run toward the caller before he turns around to look at them.
5. The players must freeze in their positions when the caller turns to face them and calls out, "Red light."
6. If the caller catches someone moving, that player must return to the starting line for the next round of calls.
7. The object of this game is for everyone to move closer to the caller on each turn until one player is able to tag him.
8. After a player tags the caller, everyone runs back to try to cross the line they started from.
9. The caller, after being tagged, turns around and tries to tag the players before they cross the line.
10. If the caller tags a player, that player becomes the caller.
11. If a player drops a ball during the drill, he must return to the starting line.

KEY POINTS

This is a fun practice break. It is also great for preseason indoor practice where there might not be enough space for conventional baseball drills. This game serves a variety of purposes in a youth baseball practice.

1. It teaches players to squeeze their gloves so that they don't drop the ball.

2. Players grow accustomed to running with their baseball gloves on.

3. It provides a great break during a hard practice.

4. Coaches can participate in the drill by taking a turn as a runner or caller.

5. The game should not be played for points; it would take too much time. But you can use this game to determine the order for batting practice. For example, the first four people who tag the caller and run safely past the starting line can be the first up at batting practice. Or those four could receive a couple of extra swings during batting practice. Rewarding players who succeed at different drills keeps players motivated during other drills.

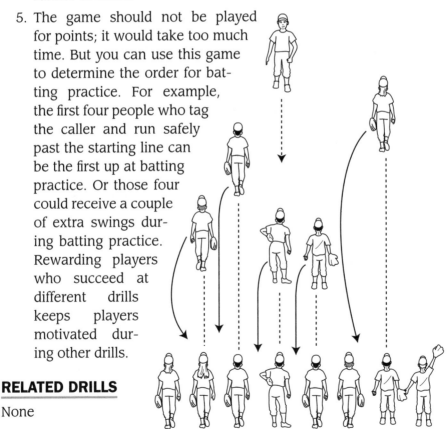

RELATED DRILLS

None

HOME-RUN DERBY

74

PURPOSE
To end practice on a high note

EQUIPMENT
Four bases, a bucket of baseballs, a fence or some cones

TIME
This game is so popular, it can be played anywhere from 10 to 20 minutes.

PROCEDURE
1. Place three bases (or four depending on the age of the participants) five to eight feet apart from one another in a straight line toward second base.
2. Each base represents home plate. Older players use the base farthest from second as home plate, while younger hitters stand at the base closest to second.
3. Players scatter around the field to field the balls.
4. The coach pitches a predetermined number of balls from shallow center field.
5. If a player hits the ball over the fence, it is a home run. The batter gets an extra swing for every home run.
6. If there is no fence, set up a boundary with cones.

KEY POINTS
1. Players having trouble hitting the ball over the fence may move up to the closest home plate.
2. This is the only drill where players are encouraged to hit home runs.
3. Coaches should not be concerned with the quality of a player's swing. This drill is primarily a fun exercise to break up or finish a practice.
4. Point out good fielding plays during this drill. Positive reinforcement is important because it emphasizes that, even in

fun drills, mastering the fundamentals is the key to a successful baseball team.

5. If very few home runs are being hit, move the bases closer to the outfield grass.

Variations

Encourage every player to swing for the fences.

1. Players can also use a tennis racket to hit tennis balls.

2. The batters can swing with one or two hands.

3. The coach can move in closer and pitch underhand to improve the batters' chance of hitting home runs.

RELATED DRILLS

None

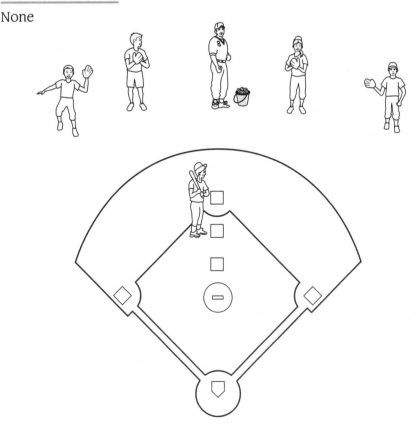

HOLE IN THE DIAMOND

PURPOSE

To teach fielders to keep hard-hit balls in front them

EQUIPMENT

A bucket of baseballs, a bat, gloves

TIME

3 to 6 minutes

PROCEDURE

1. Divide the players into four teams of three, assuming there are 12 available players. Players have their gloves with them.
2. One team spreads out between first and second base.
3. Another team spreads out between second and third base.
4. Both teams situate themselves halfway between the infield and the outfield grass.
5. The two other teams stand in the outfield and back up the first two teams.
6. The coach hits a baseball to the team on one side of the diamond.
7. The infielders try to prevent the baseball from reaching the outfield grass.
8. The coach then hits a baseball to the team on the other side of the diamond.
9. If the ball reaches the outfield grass, the other team receives one point.
10. Each infield team fields four to six balls, then rotates with the teams in the outfield.

KEY POINTS

Fielding the ball does not necessarily mean making the catch. Keeping the ball in front of the body can be just as effective.

1. Teach fielders to try to catch each ball. However, if they can't, they can save runs simply by staying in front of the ball and slowing its movement.

2. Some players might want to dive to keep the ball from going into the outfield; the coach must decide whether this should be allowed.

3. Players should watch the ball go into the glove.

RELATED DRILLS

3, 10, 15

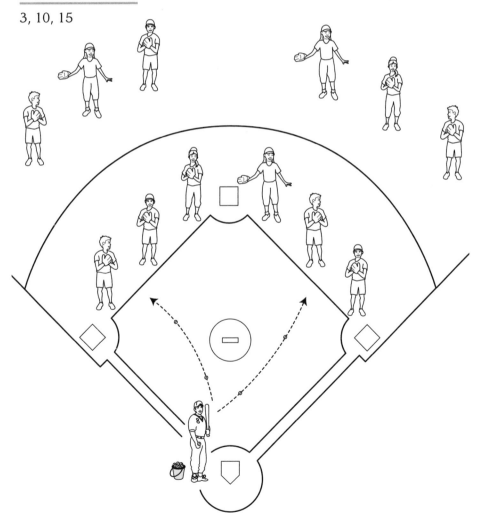

76   FOOTBALL BASEBALL

PURPOSE

To reward a good practice

EQUIPMENT

Cones, two baseballs per player, a few tennis balls, gloves

TIME

7 to 15 minutes

PROCEDURE

1. Divide the team into two groups.
2. Set up cones in a rectangular shape to resemble a small football field.
3. Four players on each team move to separate ends of the field. Each team has two substitutes.
4. This game is similar to touch or flag football, except played with a tennis ball instead of a football. There are no kickoffs or extra points in this game.
5. The coach starts the game at the estimated 20-yard line.
6. The defensive team holds two baseballs each in their gloves. The offensive team members' gloves are empty so they can catch the ball.
7. When a player on the offensive team completes a pass with the tennis ball, the defensive players try to tag him with their gloves.
8. If one of the baseballs falls out of the defensive player's glove during the tag, the play continues until another player can make the tag.
9. The coach can determine whether teams have three or four plays to make a touchdown. There are no first downs.
10. When a team scores a touchdown, the other team begins with the ball at the estimated 20-yard line.
11. The coach is the referee and should have a whistle.

KEY POINTS

This is one of the most popular games for breaking up a tough practice.

1. Players should squeeze the balls tightly in their gloves.
2. Many traditional games can be changed to include a baseball theme. Challenge the players to come up with one or two.

RELATED DRILLS

13, 18

77 ONE-PITCH BOOM BAT

PURPOSE

A fun game to reward players and involve coaches and parents

EQUIPMENT

Cones; a large plastic bat; a Wiffle ball or other large, plastic, easy-to-hit ball; gloves

TIME

5 to 10 minutes

PROCEDURE

1. Divide the players into two teams.
2. Create a large makeshift baseball diamond marked with cones.
3. The coach can pitch the ball overhand or underhand. The batter must swing at every pitch.
4. If the ball goes outside the diamond, the team gets one run.
5. If the ball is caught, goes foul, is misplayed, or does not reach the outside of the diamond, the batter is out. Therefore, every player can produce only a run or an out.
6. The fielders are not allowed to field a ball beyond the boundaries of the diamond.
7. Because the batters must swing at every pitch, each team gets five outs.

KEY POINTS

This is an easy skill game that players, coaches, and parents will enjoy.

1. Encourage players to swing for the fences, but point out that sometimes the ball travels farther if the hitter does not swing too hard.
2. Coaches should point out that teamwork and peer encouragement are important in this game. Usually this encouragement transfers to baseball games.

3. One of the best things about this game, much like home-run derby, is that players with weaker skills can be just as successful as the stronger players. When a weaker player hits a home run, make a big deal out of it to boost his confidence.

Variations

1. A variation especially appropriate for younger players is to use a beach ball and a tee.
2. Players can also run the bases.
3. Shorten the field and play the game like a home-run derby.

RELATED DRILLS

40, 75

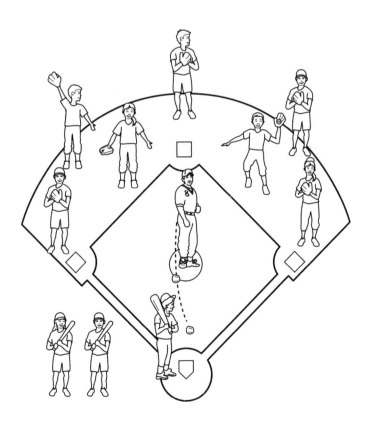

78   444 GAME (4 VS. 4 VS. 4)

PURPOSE

To play an actual game with only 12 players

EQUIPMENT

A regular playing field, balls, bats, gloves

TIME

10 to 20 minutes or a specific number of innings

PROCEDURE

1. Divide players into three teams of four players. Each team has at least one pitcher and catcher.
2. One team is at bat.
3. The other two take the field. Only two players play the outfield. One of the coaches can play an outfield position.
4. Play a normal game.
5. After the first team makes three outs, the next team is up. After they make three outs, the final team is up.

KEY POINTS

Simulating real game situations is the best way to prepare for competition, and the 444 game is a great way to do so.

1. One coach calls balls and strikes behind the pitcher.
2. Each team should have a catcher. If not, stealing might have to be suspended.
3. To keep the game moving at a fast pace, limit each team to one time through its lineup (four at-bats).
4. To familiarize players with starting behind the count, start each player off with two strikes (0-2).
5. This game is a great opportunity to try players at different positions.

RELATED DRILLS

45, 75

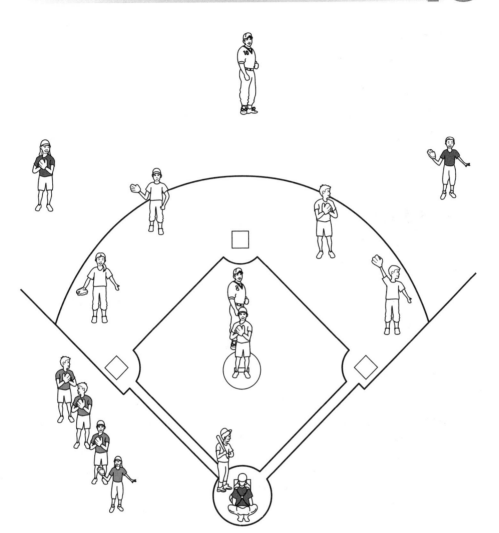

79   SCRAMBLE THE EGG

PURPOSE

To teach or reinforce bunting techniques

EQUIPMENT

A bucket of very old baseballs, a bat, a dozen eggs, a clear plastic tarp

TIME

8 to 12 minutes

PROCEDURE

1. Lay out the tarp on the ground and place the eggs on top of it.
2. The first player bunts the ball toward the eggs, with the goal of trying to break or "scramble" the eggs with the ball.
3. Give each player several chances, but make sure there are enough eggs to last the entire drill.

KEY POINTS

This is messy but incredibly fun. Only do this drill once, usually at the end of the season when the baseballs you have been using are worn out.

1. The player should square to bunt when the pitcher's front foot is about to hit the ground.
2. Substitute water balloons for eggs; however, they are harder to break.
3. Make sure the players are away from the tarp when the coach cleans up.

RELATED DRILLS

41, 43

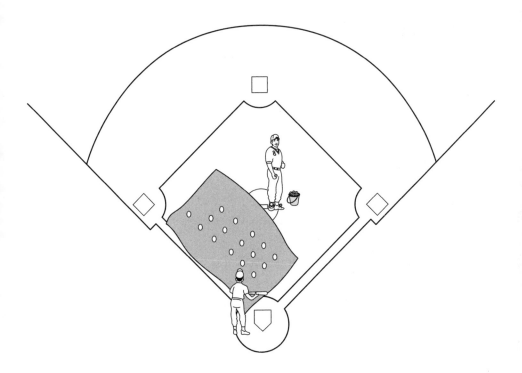

80   MAKE A RAG BALL

PURPOSE

To provide an alternative to using a hardball for some drills

EQUIPMENT

A box of rags, rolls of masking tape

TIME

5 to 10 minutes

PROCEDURE

1. Distribute the rags among the players, keeping one rag to use for demonstration.
2. Tie a large knot in the center of the rag.
3. Wrap or crumple the loose ends around the center knot to give the rag ball shape.
4. Wrap the masking tape around the rag. Make sure to cover all exposed parts of the rag.

KEY POINTS

This item can be used over and over again and is a great alternative to spending large amounts of money on equipment.

1. The masking tape should not be applied too tight. If it's too tight the rag ball will have too much bounce.
2. Coaches can use these rag balls in many drills, including the Racquetball Drill and the Toss Drill.
3. Over the course of the season, the rag ball will get worn out. Instead of throwing it out, simply apply more layers of tape on top of the existing layers.

Variation

Some coaches may want to use old newspaper as an alternative to rags. This works well; however, additional masking tape is necessary to give the ball its needed weight.

RELATED DRILLS

11, 36

Sample Practices

Conducting a successful practice is not complicated as long as you have spent time in the preseason planning. This preparation allows you to run a crisp, upbeat, one-hour practice that covers the fundamentals. Remember, a practice of more than an hour and fifteen minutes is not necessary for baseball players 7 to 12 years old. A well-organized practice should include five to eight drills, with one or two backup drills in case the team does not respond to some of the planned exercises.

Start the practice with one or two warm-up drills. After the warm-ups is a good time to gather the team to review the last game and to go over what they will do during the day's practice. It is also a good time to point out player's achievements in the last game. Point out two or three players at each practice and make sure to mention everyone during the season. Even the weakest player can make up for a lack of natural talent with hustle, and the coach should point this out.

The main goal of each practice is to actively involve as many players as possible in every drill. This limits downtime, where players would otherwise stand around watching. The coach, therefore, must use assistant coaches to run several drills at the same time, focusing on different skills. Even during a regular batting practice you can set up two on-deck stations with one player using a batting tee and the other player working on the toss drill with a coach.

Assistant coaches are an important part of a youth baseball team. When choosing an assistant coach, do not simply go with the parent who shows up early for a game or stays to watch the team's practices. The assistant coach should be someone who has had experience coaching or is eager to learn. It should be someone who can naturally step in to coach if you cannot make a game or practice. Brief the assistant coach, or coaches, at the beginning of the season on what you want to accomplish and some of the ways you will teach the numerous baseball skills to the players. Encourage the assistant coaches to voice their opinions and ideas.

A well-rounded practice should include basic drills and skill-oriented drills as well as work on strategy. And don't forget to include a warm-up or cool-down drill or two to break up the practice. However, once you have designed the "perfect" practice, remember that it can be changed. Think of your practice as having a flexible structure. Plan to go over certain drills, but be prepared to deviate if necessary. For instance, if a drill works extremely well and players want more repetition, extend this drill. On the other hand, if a drill just isn't working, move on to something else.

Mix things up once in a while and hold a mini batting practice or play your team's favorite drill at the beginning of practice. These are great strategies for making sure players arrive at practice on time.

The following are guidelines for designing a practice session:

1. Cover one or two individual or team skills in each practice.
2. Practices should last no longer than 75 minutes.
3. Use your assistant coaches. For example, they can work with individuals on the toss drill off to the side.
4. The key to an effective practice is for all players to be active during the allotted time.

Outdoor Practices

Outdoor practices are the most important and practical type of practice. If your league or community is fortunate enough to provide ample fields for practices, make the most of this time and space. Players learn more during good outdoor practices than during games. However, many leagues do not have enough fields, or field time is limited. Therefore, prepare for practice well before the team steps on the field. And be prepared to practice even if you are bumped to a corner of the field. In this case, be prepared with backup drills suited for smaller spaces.

Before every practice, make sure you have one or two backup drills ready in case the planned drills aren't working or there are not enough players to complete one of the drills. Developing a master list of drills at the beginning of the season and categorizing them saves significant time during the season and makes for more efficient practices. List the drills and their allotted time on an index card. List alternate drills on the back of the card.

Outdoor Practice 1 (baserunning emphasis)

1. Third-base drill, 6 to 8 minutes (#3)
2. Read the sign, 6 to 8 minutes (#55)
3. First-and-third offensive situation, 6 to 8 minutes (#63)
4. Circle drill, 6 to 8 minutes (#17)
5. Tagging up, 6 to 8 minutes (#53)
6. Bounce and run, 6 to 8 minutes (#54)
7. Bunt drill batting practice, 6 to 8 minutes (#42)
8. Batting practice, 10 to 15 minutes (chapter 3)

In this practice, three drills are devoted to baserunning, which is one of the most underrated skills in youth baseball. Coaches should incorporate at least one baserunning drill at each practice. This practice includes a warm-up or cool-down drill between two skill drills. Youth players do not have long attentions spans; therefore, fun drills contribute to a smoother, more successful practice.

Outdoor Practice 2

1. Mini batting practice, 4 to 6 minutes (chapter 3)
2. Bounce and run, 6 to 8 minutes (#54)
3. Around the horn, 6 to 8 minutes (#19)
4. Wild pitch, 6 to 8 minutes (#22)
5. First and third defensive situation and backing up, 8 to 10 minutes (#64)
6. Bunt-drill batting practice, 6 to 8 minutes (#42)
7. Batting practice using a hitting drill, 10 to 15 minutes (chapter 3)
8. Football baseball, 10 to15 minutes (#76)

Batting practice can be used as a great motivator, even for very young players, at any practice. Coaches can give players a number upon their arrival to practice, and their number will determine when they will bat during batting practice. This method is a great way to get players to practice on time. A mini batting practice can also begin a team practice once in a while in order to ensure the timely arrival by all. Batting practice itself can be run in a number of ways. Remember that only one player can bat, so the coach needs to concern himself with getting as many players involved and keep the batting practice moving in a spirited, safe manner. During batting practice, one of the safety concerns of the coach is that players will be running in and out of the playing field once they have hit or are about to hit. A great way to run batting practice with 10, 11, or 12 players is to have two on-deck batters. One of the on-deck batters (it must be the "double on-deck batter") can hit off the batting tee on the other side of the fence or in a safe area. Or an assistant coach can practice the Toss Drill. The on-deck batter should always be ready to go into the batter's box as soon as the previous hitter is done. Once the hitter has taken his last swing, he will grab his glove and run to a position on the field. Another player will run in from the field and become the double on-deck batter. Coaches should limit the swings to five or six but can also reward players with extra swings. For example, if a player successfully bunts the first two pitches fair, then he receives two extra swings. Coaches should be creative with batting practice and can put in fun exercises, such as giving the batters an extra swing for every ball hit fair to the right side, left of second base, or whichever side the coach decides to designate. Coaches should always utilize their assistant coaches in all drills, but it is imperative that these assistants know the safety concerns of batting practice.

The order of these drills is not important. In fact, except for the warm-up drills, the order in which you schedule drills should vary from practice to practice. Sometimes it's appropriate to place the skill drills at the beginning of practice, for example, if there was a game the day before and you need to give immediate attention to a situation from that game. At other times you'll place them in the middle. Or if you have a game the next day, practice them at the end so that the players go home with a particular drill fresh in their minds. The only common denominator in youth practices is to include a warm-up or cool-down drill or activity after one or two teaching drills or skills. And always end on a high note, either with a batting practice or a cool-down drill.

Kids are smart; therefore, you must avoid predictable practices. Otherwise, after a fun warm-up drill, they will talk among themselves, complaining about which "hard" drill they might have to do next. Another tactic for keeping practice interesting is to rotate to different parts of the field for each drill. Moving to a different location keeps the drills and the players fresh. Competition also keeps players involved in practice. Kids love competitive games, so make many of your drills a competition or a challenge. For instance, divide the team in half during the lead drill, and whichever team makes the most catches wins. Don't be afraid to be creative. If you have a brainstorm for a new drill or variation, try it. It's OK to deviate from your original practice schedule.

Outdoor Practice 3 (defensive emphasis)

1. Long toss, 4 to 6 minutes (#47)
2. Third-base drill, 6 to 8 minutes (#3)
3. First-and-third offensive and defensive situations, 8 to 12 minutes (#63, #64)
4. Bounce and run, 6 to 8 minutes (#54)
5. Lead drill, 4 to 6 minutes (#13)
6. Desperation throw, 4 to 6 minutes (#29)
7. Three-man relay, 4 to 6 minutes (#8)
8. Bunt-drill batting practice, 6 to 8 minutes (#42)
9. Home-run derby, 6 to 10 minutes (#74)

This practice at its longest lasts only 70 minutes. The majority of time should be spent on the first-and-third situational drill and the bounce-and-run baserunning drill. Ending the practice with a home-run derby gives the players something to look forward to. If there is no fence, set up a boundary with cones. If players are very young, use a tennis racket and tennis ball for the home-run derby. Everyone shows up for the following practice when you end a practice with a home-run derby.

Outdoor Practice 4

1. Third-base drill, 4 to 6 minutes (#3)
2. Wild pitch, 4 to 6 minutes (#22)
3. Toss drill (three stations), 8 to 12 minutes (#36)
4. Around the horn, 6 to 8 minutes (#19)
5. Bounce and run, 8 to 12 minutes (#54)

6. Baserunning drills: Home to second, first to third, second to home, 10 to 16 minutes (#56, #57, #58)

7. Situation drills using a game situation drill, 8 to 12 minutes (chapter 6)

8. Bunt-drill batting practice, 6 to 8 minutes (#42)

9. Batting practice using a hitting drill, 8 to 15 minutes (chapter 3)

In this practice several baserunning and bunting drills are repeated from the other practices. Baserunning and bunting, when applied correctly, can produce up to three extra runs per game. This is a long and challenging practice; however, you have the flexibility to decrease the time for any of these drills. Before every practice, make sure you have one or two backup drills ready in case the scheduled drills aren't working or there are not enough players to complete one of the drills.

Outdoor Practice 5

1. Continuation drill, 8 to 10 minutes (#44)

2. Batting practice, 12 to 20 minutes

3. Any warm-up or cool-down game, 10 to 15 minutes

This practice provides a change of pace from those described previously. Hold a practice like this occasionally, particularly if the team plays many games in a row or if they seem to be flat. Announce ahead of time that the team will have a special short practice of batting and warm-up and cool-down drills only. Remember, batting practice is extremely popular with players, so do not deny them. But make sure it is creative and fun.

Parking Lot Practices

Many times a coach calls a practice only to find one or more teams using the field he had intended to use. Because there is a shortage of practice fields around the country, plan a backup practice with drills your team can perform effectively in a parking lot. These drills must take into account the limited space and must be the type of drills that are safe and useful on concrete. Common sense is imperative: Eliminate any drill involving sliding or diving, and replace hardballs with tennis balls and soft-covered balls. Always have them available in case you need to hold practice in a parking lot. When playing with tennis balls, it is sometimes better to practice without gloves; tennis balls tend to bounce out of gloves. If players use gloves anyway, tell them not to concern themselves too much if they have trouble controlling the tennis balls.

Parking-lot practices should focus on skills and drills that can be practiced in confined areas, such as bunting, catching fly balls, the toss drill, and numerous warm-up and cool-down games. Setting up different stations is an effective strategy for these practices. Parking lot practices can be more difficult to run; however, they can be just as successful as field practices.

Parking Lot Practice 1

1. Third-base drill (with tennis or soft-covered ball), 8 to 10 minutes (#3)
2. Rundown drill (with tennis or soft-covered ball), 8 to 10 minutes (#24)
3. Running bases (with tennis or soft-covered ball), 6 to 8 minutes (chapter 3)
4. Read the sign (with tennis or soft-covered ball), 6 to 8 minutes (#55)
5. Circle drill (with tennis or soft-covered ball), 6 to 8 minutes (#17)
6. Home-run derby (with tennis ball and tennis racket), 10 to 15 minutes (#74)

Parking Lot Practice 2

1. Line master (with tennis or soft-covered ball), 8 to 10 minutes (#5)
2. Toss and tee-ball drills (three or four stations using a wall or fence), 12 to 16 minutes (#36, #37)
3. Three man–relay (with tennis or soft-covered ball), 6 to 10 minutes (#8)
4. One-pitch boom bat, 8 to 12 minutes (#77)

Indoor Practices

Indoor practices, usually held in a school gym, are common during the preseason, especially in cold-weather areas. These practices should be just as stimulating and educational as outdoor practices. You may have to include a few more warm-up drills; however, a well-planned indoor practice can be very effective, especially if you use numerous stations simultaneously. For example, some players can hit a rag ball against the wall in one station as other players work off of the batting tee in another station. The coach, as well as the league, must verify with school districts that indoor practices are allowed and what types of drills are prohibited. Many schools frown on the use of hardballs on a gym floor.

Some communities have batting-cage facilities, which are excellent for indoor practices. However, because many families might not be able to afford the fees, coaches and leagues should develop policies regarding the monetary cost. If you decide to use a batting cage, you are better off renting two cages for a half hour than one cage for an hour. Players get restless waiting for their turn, and two cages cuts the wait time in half. Some hitting facilities also have gyms, which allows players to work on other drills in the gym while they wait for their turn in the batting cage.

Indoor Practice 1

1. Circle drill (with tennis or soft-covered ball), 6 to 8 minutes (#17)
2. Toss and tee-ball drills (three or four stations using a wall), 12 to 16 minutes (#36, #37)
3. One-knee drill (with tennis or soft-covered ball), 6 to 8 minutes (#50)
4. Running bases (with tennis or soft-covered ball), 6 to 8 minutes (chapter 5)
5. Goalie drill (with tennis or soft-covered ball), 6 to 8 minutes (#10)
6. Read the sign (with tennis or soft-covered ball), 6 to 8 minutes (#55)

7. One-pitch boom bat (or Wiffle-ball game), 8 to 12 minutes (#77)

Indoor Practice 2

1. Line throw (with tennis or soft-covered ball), 6 to 8 minutes

2. Toss and tee-ball drills (three or four stations using a wall or fence), 12 to 16 minutes (#36, #37)

3. Run at base runner, 6 to 8 minutes (#23)

4. Read the sign (with tennis or soft-covered ball), 6 to 8 minutes (chapter 5)

5. Running bases (with tennis or soft-covered ball), 6 to 8 minutes (chapter 5)

6. One-pitch boom bat (or Wiffle-ball game), 8 to 12 minutes (#77)

Ten Tips for Youth Coaches

Over the years, I have developed certain youth practice principles that have contributed to smoother and more successful seasons. These principles move beyond baseball skills to address player motivation, team cohesiveness, administrative logistics, and parental involvement.

1. Hold a mandatory parents meeting before the first practice to let parents know what is expected of everyone during the season. Supply handouts and keep the meeting brief.

2. Buy a trophy (and make it a big one) before the first practice. Award this Tenth Player Award at the end of the season to the player who exhibited the most spirit and helped the coaches carry equipment during the season. This award has nothing to do with a player's ability.

3. Appoint a "team parent" to coordinate a network of communication with other parents and with players.

4. Set up a phone chain to communicate practice changes, rain-outs, and so forth.

5. Ask players to bring their own water bottles with their names on them to every practice and game.

6. Hand out a list of equipment that every player should have. In the last few years, parents have started buying their children their own batting helmets. Players are encouraged to buy their own equipment as long as it complies with league rules.

7. Mark all team and individual bats (get the parent's permission). Stick the knob of the bat through a piece of cardboard and spray paint the surface of the knob a particular color. Leagues can even institute this idea and assign a particular color to each team. This makes it easier to identify team bats and cuts down on mix-ups with other teams.

8. Give players numbers as they arrive at practice to designate in what order they will hit in batting practice. This encourages players to arrive at practice on time.

9. Put out a team newsletter every three or four weeks; mention each player at least once during the year. One page is sufficient. A team parent can be in charge of this, but the coach should read it over before distributing it.

10. Hold a team picnic or party at the end of the season. At the party, speak about individual and team improvements during the season. Call up each player and say something positive. Also recognize team parents who helped throughout the season.

About the Author

Coach Marty Schupak is the founder and president of the Youth Sports Club, a group dedicated to improving Little League coaching and youth baseball. His Web site, www.youthsportsclub.com, has become one of the most frequented resources for youth coaches and parents.

Over the past 15 years, Schupak has managed or coached more than 1,200 kids in youth athletics with teams winning over 200 games and a host of championships. Many of his former players and students have gone on to successful high school baseball careers and athletic college scholarships. In addition to coaching baseball, Schupak has coached children in basketball and soccer. He has served on the board of directors of various leagues and organizations, including the American Baseball Coaches Association.

Schupak has written numerous articles on youth sports and developed the best-selling baseball video *The 59 Minute Baseball Practice* as well as *Backyard Baseball Drills, Winning Baseball Strategies, 48 Championship Basketball Drills, Pitching Drills & Techniques,* and *Championship Soccer Drills.* He received a bachelor's degree from Boston University in 1975 and a master's degree in physical education from Arizona State University in 1978. Schupak lives in Valley Cottage, New York.